A Pastor's Devotion

To Angie;
May the Lord bless
you always.
Pastor Mason
July 22, 2022
Dogwood Valley
Camp

A Pastor's Devotion

Francis Mason

ISBN 978-1-68517-599-3 (paperback)
ISBN 978-1-68517-600-6 (digital)

Christian Faith Publishing
832 Park Avenue
Meadville, PA 16335
www.christianfaithpublishing.com

Printed in the United States of America

These selected devotions were written by a Pastor to his congregation during the time of governmental pandemic restrictions, preventing them from gathering for purposes of worship and prayer.

Written for encouragement and with the intent that his daily submissions be uplifting, it soon became evident they would also be useful in creating a bridge for communication between the pulpit and pew during an unusually long and hurtful cycle of silence from the comfortable environment of the sanctuary. Christian principles and truths were transmitted daily in a variety of formats—sometimes humorous, serious, intellectual, country colloquial, sophisticated, and theological. Paul said it this way: "I am made all things to all men that I might by all means save some."

It is the author's desire that you would be both encouraged and strengthened as you read these expressions of the heart from the heart of a Pastor.

~ ~ ~ ~ ~ ~ ~ ~ ~ ~ ~ ~ ~ ~ ~ ~ ~ ~ ~ ~

Special thanks go to those who helped in so many ways, especially with tech problems having to do with setup and style. My sweet granddaughter Hollie Harris Groulx, nursing assistant at St. Joseph's Hospital, Bellingham, Washington; Felipe Rodrigues, third year student at Urshan College; and Esosa Aimiose, third year engineering student at BCIT. These were willing to go deep into the woods of computer know-how and help me find my way when I couldn't do it no how.

Having rights and privileges to a special place in my heart is Gloria, the little girl whose raven's wing hair has turned into a mantle of silvery snow during the sixty-one years of being called my girl friend. In more ways than can be numbered, she is my friend. To her belongs the accolades and a heartfelt Thank You once again.

This book of devotional writings is affectionately dedicated to the memory of three beautiful ladies who made lasting impressions upon my life. My beautiful mother, Nancy Viola Mason, was a lover of God and the people of God. Among the many events of the church, she loved to read articles written by our ministers. In her later years, after father was gone, I would gather up various church magazines, Sunday bulletins, missionary newsletters, etc. and send her a bundle for her reading enjoyment. She went to be with Dad and her Lord Jesus just before the COVID-19 pandemic. Oh, how she would have loved to be on my mailing list to receive these daily devotionals.

Phyllis Jardine was a beautiful saint of God from Chipman, New Brunswick, whom God sent to British Columbia after her retirement from teaching and being principal of a high school. She was a preacher's friend. Unafraid to speak her mind, she would often give expression to her observations and opinions with a wit and wisdom that was a blessing to be received from the pew. When she began developing aches and pains, she will forever be remembered for saying, "Getting old isn't for cowards."

Mrs. Marjorie Cairns, English teacher extraordinaire, helped this young high-school student "bookworm" to love words—their structure, their power, their beauty. In her southern accented speech, she taught me to enunciate distinctly, to speak expressively, and to love my mother tongue.

Disclaimers and Invitations

In collecting material for use in my writings, I have tried to give credit where it was possible to do so. Over many years, I have gathered material "precept upon precept; line upon line; here a little, and there a little" (Isaiah 28:10). Often, I know not whence it came or from whom. May God bless all the "Unknown Authors" and Sources Unknown for their unheralded assistance here. No claims of absolute originality are made for this material.

All scripture references are taken from the King James Version of the Bible (KJV) unless noted otherwise by abbreviated designation listed here:

- AMPC—Amplified Bible (Classic)
- CEV—Contemporary English Version
- DRB—Darby Bible
- ESV—English Standard Version
- GNB—Good News Bible
- MSG—The Message
- NIV—New International Version
- Wey—Weymouth New Testament

There is a delightful little Greek restaurant called New York, New York located near my home in Newton, which my wife and I frequent from time to time; and I have a marvelously funny story about something that happened to me at Mars Hill in Athens while visiting there as a tourist. I'd be happy to tell you about it sometime should you ask; but that is the extent of my knowledge of Greek. I know that Paul (I think it was Paul) who wrote a rather deep and sometimes hard to understand book in the New Testament, giving it the name of Hebrews. That's about as close as I've come to reading Hebrew. Other than that, I don't.

Respectfully yours,
Francis William Mason
August 20, 2021

Can You See the Ark?

Thy raiment waxed not old upon thee, neither did thy foot swell, these forty years. Beware that thou forget not the LORD thy God, in not keeping his commandments, and his judgments, and his statutes, which I command thee this day: And thou say in thine heart, My power and the might of mine hand hath gotten me this wealth. But thou shalt remember the LORD thy God: for it is he that giveth thee power to get wealth, that he may establish his covenant which he sware unto thy fathers, as it is this day.

—Deuteronomy 8:4, 11, 17–18

As the dawn is breaking forth upon a new day and a new year, the instructions of God to Joshua crossing the Jordan comes to mind: "When you see the ark of the covenant of the Lord your God being borne by the Levitical priests, set out from where you are and follow it. Yet a space must be kept between you and it, about 2000 cubits by measure; come not near it, that you may [be able to see the ark and] know the way you must go, for you have not passed this way before" (Joshua 3:3–4 AMP).

This simple explanation about the distancing between the people and the ark should suffice—i.e., if the people overcrowd around the ark, those nearest it would cause it to be lost to the sight of the others following behind. The purpose of this visible evidence of Jehovah was to provide divine leadership for all of Israel.

More than understanding the need for keeping the Ark of the Covenant visible to all the people, the main thrust and intended object of instruction is to impress upon the minds of the people the supremacy of God. It was God that caused the feet of the wilderness travelers to not swell from all the walking they did over a forty-year span. Their clothing and their sandals did not become old and worn out. In other words, God was saying, "I've taken care of you all these years. I won't stop now!"

Beware that you not forget the LORD thy God. Perhaps the lesson needing the greatest attention by the Israelites (and us) is the lesson about resources. Where do I get my provision from? Who is my supplier? Who puts money in my bank account? (Bear with me for a moment). Who gave me the job that I have? There are others who don't have a job. Where do my strength, my knowledge, my skill come from? If you say in your heart, "My power and the might of mine hand has gotten me this wealth, then thou shalt remember the LORD thy God: for it is he that giveth thee power to get wealth."

The song says, "He woke me up this morning and started me on my way." Just remember, God did it!

He woke you up! Happy New Year!

You're My Brother...
More than Words

Behold, how good and how pleasant it is for brethren to dwell together in unity! It is like the precious ointment upon the head, that ran down upon the beard, even Aaron's beard: that went down to the skirts of his garments; As the dew of Hermon, and as the dew that descended upon the mountains of Zion: for there the LORD commanded the blessing, even life for evermore.

—Psalm 133:1–3

With the appearance of a great monolithic gate stands the Peace Arch astride the border of Canada and the United States of America. Cast into the structural form of the monument are the words of Psalm 133:1: "Brethren Dwelling Together In Unity." The message, of course, is obvious. Less obvious to the viewers eyes is a symbolic gate between the two gigantic legs of the monument. Inscribed above the gate are the words "May These Gates Never Be Closed."

The brotherhood is not a unity of sameness. God never makes the brothers of a family alike. And when he remakes men, he does not shape them to a pattern; rather, he gives them a new common life. The oil is not presented as stopping with intellectual people who are often adjudged to be the head; it goes on downward to the hem of Aaron's garment, therefore touching all people. All the members of the body retain their individualities but are represented as being touched by the fragrant flow of the good and pleasant unity of brotherhood.

The brotherhood is a unity of grace received. The new bond uniting all the members of the body and all the relations of the life (which are represented by the garments) is the oil of divine grace, which reaches to and sanctifies us all.

The brotherhood is a unity of common response. Every part gives forth fragrance, and it is everywhere the same fragrance of that godly character and godly living, which grace sanctifies. Scents are dependent on the substances on which they lie. Some absorb and destroy fragrance. Others freely give it forth. The unity of the Church is the fragrance of the holy living of each one of its members.

The unity of the Church is the unity of brethren. They feel that they have a common Father and are children of the same household. But it is unity in variety—variety of thought but unity of heart, a unity of the utmost extremes from the head to the edge of the garments of society from the heights of Hermon to the more humble hill of Zion.

There is another side of unity to be considered today. Not only are our thoughts forming around the importance of cross-border harmony but in the multicultural, multiracial mix within the boundaries of individual countries, provinces, cities; even within the framework of our own families and homes, unity can come only from love. And love is the greatest goodness and the highest, deepest joy.

True unity is the most fragrant and refreshing fact of life, in the individual and in the Church, and in society. And unity only begins to do what it is supposed to do when individuals become motivated to say, "Let me help my brother today." Indeed, let it start in me!

The King's Message

I had read about this event several years ago and barely recalled the essentials of the story. After research, I found not only the story but discovered the resource to be a well-known writer of gospel books and articles today, Mr. Warren Wiersbe. Interspersed with my own thoughts, this amazing story and some of Wiersbe's comments are presented for your blessing. It goes something like this:

> Britain's King George V was to give the opening address at a special disarmament conference with the speech relayed by radio to the United States. As the broadcast was about to begin, a cable broke in the New York radio station, and more than a million listeners were left without sound. A junior mechanic in the station, Harold Vivien, solved the problem by picking up both ends of the cable, allowing 250 volts of electricity to pass through him. He became the living link that allowed the king's message to get through.

Wow! Wiersbe said, "I almost couldn't believe it, so I did a bit more digging on Saturday night and came across this news article from *The Huntsville Daily Times*, January 21, 1930." The news reporter wrote, "His arms, twitching with shocks from electric current, Harold Vivian, a young radio engineer, literally spliced with his body a broken link in the vast hookup and made it possible for listeners on fifty-nine North American radio stations to hear King George's speech. Vivian, chief control operator, grasped the wires together in his hands to restore the circuit. Leakage of current through his body to the floor shook his arms with spasms, but he held on without a break for twenty minutes until new wires could be connected."

The king's message got through; whatever it took! And, saints, that's how we get to impact the world! The Early Church was characterized by zeal for the message of the King. Nothing could dampen the zeal of the disciples whose spiritual experiences were often the foundational substance of the writings in the book of Acts. Not persecution, not suffering, nor even death. They had a message of the death, burial, and resurrection of Jesus Christ who is, after all, the King of kings and the Lord of lords. This message is called the New Birth Message. The simplicity of it is shocking to say the least: "Ye must be born again" (John 3:7).

Because of this constant bold proclamation of the gospel to a world that stands in willful opposition to it, the Early Church faced hardships and persecution; but they were not deterred in their efforts to see that the message got out. They knew they were the link between the king and the people, the chosen conduit by which our glorious Lord chose to make the message of the kingdom known. They literally stood in the gap and picked up the cable.

Just one more comment: If your experience in the service of the Lord has grown lifeless—dull, maybe boring—should there be a broken cable lying about, pick it up and let the King's message flow uninterrupted through you to hungry hearts. They will get the message, and your experience will be electrifying, to say the least.

The World's Smallest Bible

Then shalt thou call, and the LORD shall answer;
thou shalt cry, and He shall say, Here I am.

—Isaiah 58:9

God did tempt Abraham, and said unto him,
"Abraham:" and he said, "Behold, here I am."
And Isaac spake unto Abraham and said, "My
father:" and he said, "Here am I, my son."

—Genesis 22:1, 7

The world's smallest Bible fits on the tip of a pen. Scientists
etched 1.2 million letters onto a tiny silicon disk covered in gold,
then with a focused ion beam to engrave the letters one at a time,
they blasted away the gold to reveal the darker silicon beneath. But
to read this tiny Old Testament, you'd need a very big microscope.
If you want to check the work, you'd have to magnify the font about
ten thousand times. They're calling it the Nano Bible, and reading it
would require an electron microscope.

Yet the message of the Bible may be encompassed in its entirety
in three of the shortest words contained in it: "Here Am I." Properly
understood and used, these words include all things required by God
and needed for man.

In our first text found in Isaiah 58:9, the words were said by
God to man; in text number two, by man to God; and in the third
text, they were spoken by man to man. Therefore, we may consider

that they sum up that which comes from God that which goes to God and that which is done for God.

"Why art thou cast down, O my soul? and why art thou disquieted in me? hope thou in God: for I shall yet praise him for the help of his countenance. Deep calleth unto deep at the noise of thy waterspouts: all thy waves and thy billows are gone over me. Why art thou cast down, O my soul? and why art thou disquieted within me? hope thou in God: for I shall yet praise him, who is the health of my countenance, and my God" (Psalm 42:5, 7, 11). Notice the addition of the change caused by hope. He is the health of our outlook—our God!

This Psalm contains a prescription for a downcast soul, consisting of three ingredients. The first ingredient is inquiry. Figure it out. Pray it through. What has you down? "Why art thou cast down?" Despondency must have a cause; and if we can discover it in any case, the old proverb holds good that "knowledge of the disease is half its cure." The deep of man's need calls out to the deep of God's supply—ignoring the noise of the waterfall—which just happens to be God's supply flowing toward you!

We are given an illustration of a Chinese theologian comparing Confucius, Buddha, and Jesus Christ. He tells of a man who fell into a deep well, only to discover that Confucius ignored him in his condition. Buddha was sympathetic, but he passed him by. "But Jesus," said the theologian, "has a rope long enough to pull him out." David put it this way: "I waited and waited and waited for GOD. At last he looked; finally he listened. He lifted me out of the ditch, pulled me from deep mud. He stood me up on a solid rock to make sure I wouldn't slip" (Psalm 40:1–2 MSG).

The second ingredient of the prescription is remembrance. David remembers his own experiences with God and those of God's gracious dealings with others. He is a faithful God.

The third ingredient is hope. "Hope thou in God, for I shall yet praise Him." The hope is to be in God. The downcast soul must hope in God and not in change of circumstance. Wow! Hope is a different thing from faith, yet God causes them to work together, and hope maketh not ashamed. And I'm remembering that "all things work together for my good."

Marvelous, Monotonous, Mysterious

In his inimitable and unique manner, Vance Havner postulated in his little book, *Seasonings*, that human character faces three major tests in its journey here. The test of the marvelous comes during the great days when we are on the mountaintop of great success. A special grace is needed for these times because we tend to grow proud and drunken with the wine of victory.

The test of the monotonous—the daily grind—takes its toll through the rigor mortis of the routine. Weeks and months go by without a break in the doldrums of sameness. Someone aptly stated that the problem of the Christian's daily walk is that it is so daily.

"But the greatest test of all," wrote Havner, "is the test of the mysterious." When things happen that don't make sense; when it seems that God has forgotten us; when nothing seems to work out according to our little plans; yes, indeed, when instead of a storybook ending, everything collapses in chaos and confusion—that's when our brow wrinkles in wonderment, and we are made to exclaim, "What's going on?" It's a mystery.

We observe that Paul had been tested in all these levels. He had personal knowledge of the exaltation of the third heaven (the marvelous), the daily care of the churches (the monotonous), and the thorn in the flesh (the mysterious). It seems so easy to assume that a special "apostolic dispensation" carried Paul through; but like us, he was mere human. It is good to be apostolic, but these mysterious events are your dispensation right now!

God has chosen to position himself at every one of these stations of life. He surrounds us with His presence everywhere. In his omnipresence, he is found to ride "upon the heaven in thy help and in His excellency on the sky." Be it mountaintop or valley, the miraculous or the monotonous, God is there. But perhaps the most reassuring of all is knowing that even when we don't understand, and life has presented us with the mysterious, His support is still there. God is above, beneath, before, and behind us. "The eternal God is thy refuge, and underneath are the everlasting arms."

Considering the present worldwide events that are washing up on the shores of your life like a tsunami, it would be easy to feel the sudden stress of the mysterious and ask, "Why?" It might even be tempting to hide in a closet of fear and panic. (If you've had to quarantine, then you've been in a closet of mandated restrictions.) But take note of the blessed assurance given from the Lord:

> Hast thou not known? Hast thou not heard, that the everlasting God, the Lord, the Creator of the ends of the earth, fainteth not, neither is weary? There is no searching of his understanding. He giveth power to the faint; and to them that have no might he increaseth strength. Even the youths shall faint and be weary, and the young men shall utterly fall: But they that wait upon the Lord shall renew their strength; they shall mount up with wings as eagles; they shall run, and not be weary; and they shall walk, and not faint. (Isaiah 40:28–31)

Despite the mysterious, in the midst of the monotonous, or even when we experience the marvelous, we can know peace while surrounded by the presence of God. He rides upon the heavens in thy help. Believe it! He said, "I am the LORD, I change not."

Character, Class, and Christianity

See that ye refuse not him that speaketh. For if they escaped not who refused him that spake on earth, much more shall not we escape, if we turn away from him that speaketh from heaven: Whose voice then shook the earth: but now he hath promised, saying, Yet once more I shake not the earth only, but also heaven. And this word, 'Yet once more,' signifieth the removing of those things that are shaken, as of things that are made, that those things which cannot be shaken may remain.

—Hebrews 12:25–27

He will sift out everything without solid foundations, so that only unshakeable things will be left.

—Hebrews 12:27 TLB

The Lord often uses trials to realign us and storms to attack everything in us that can be shaken. Everybody God uses goes through experiences that cause them to let go of the temporal and take hold of the eternal. Some wake up in hospital rooms with beeping monitors to discover that the things they thought were important mean nothing at all. Others discover it when the person they thought was everything walks away and leaves them. Job went through it. One day, he had everything; and the next day, nothing. His health was in shambles, his children dead, and his marriage a joke. At times like that, you discover what's meant by "things which cannot be shaken" that are worth living for.

Character is not what you know; it's what you are. Class doesn't show in what you have; it shows in the way you act and even more in the way you react. Christianity is not a culture; it's a way of life. It's seeking to be Christlike, not just to observe rules and impress people but to please him. That's why Paul called it "the high calling of God in Christ Jesus."

God said, "Behold, I will do a new thing; now it shall spring forth" (Isaiah 43:19). If God says He's going to bless you, ignore your circumstances and believe the God who cannot lie. You're too important to Him to be destroyed by a situation designed to build character and give you direction. God's grace will enable you to make it through. God proved that He can bring you out of the fire without even the smell of smoke and out of the lions' den without so much as a bite mark. If you want to know what God can do, look at what He's already done for you and start praising Him.

After feeling like you've waited forever, God will suddenly move; and if you're not ready, you'll miss Him. When the Church was born, we read, "Suddenly, there came a sound from heaven as of a rushing mighty wind, and it filled all the house where they were sitting" (Acts 2:2). When God decided to bring Paul and Silas out of prison, we read, "And suddenly there was a great earthquake…and immediately all the doors were opened" (Acts 16:26). Are you ready for God to move suddenly? Are you ready for doors to open?

God's words are creatively established on His promises. He is ready to do a new thing for you today! Get ready for it to spring forth now!

The Turn in the Road

Mary Pickford was, at one time, the most powerful woman in Hollywood. During the silent film era, she was the highest paid woman in the world. In 1916, she signed a record-breaking contract of $10,000 a week for a salary. She used her ambition and business sense to become as powerful as the men around her in a time when women were not even given a seat at the table. "I have a philosophy that I have evolved over the years," she once told her guests after dinner. "It has helped me through every heartbreak and discouragement, has stood by me through every unhappy experience." As they urged her to tell them about it, she confided to her friends her secret of calm serenity, of rising above every distressing circumstance, of going on with courage and hope no matter what happened. "What looks like the end of the road in our personal experience," she said, "is only the turn in the road, the beginning of a new and more beautiful journey. I have always tried to live by that philosophy, and it has kept me happy."

Please take note that there is no inclination on my part to lend aggrandizement nor approval to any whose lifestyle is contrary to that of a godly Christian. In this case, Canadian-born Mary Pickford held the attention of the masses for over fifty years as the very first "darling" of silent films. Her acting career notwithstanding her personal philosophies of life have merit and benefit for us today. Give them fair and equitable consideration as they are presented here.

Among her guests that evening was the editor of a national magazine, and he became more and more entranced as she talked about her philosophy of life. Here was a world-famous personality, a woman of great beauty and talent who had achieved dazzling success. She had known wealth, fame, honor, and devotion. But she had known disappointments as well. She had faced unhappiness in her personal life and bitter disillusion. Yet she had come through every experience serene and composed, radiantly sure of herself and the road ahead. Surely, the philosophy of such a woman would be interesting and helpful to others. The editor asked her to write an article for his magazine, expressing her views and beliefs.

So Mary Pickford agreed to write the article. As she began to think about what she would say, she knew that first, she would emphasize her faith in God and show how faith gave her courage to meet the trials and disappointments of life. She would explain how she looked upon unhappy experiences as a turn in the road—an end but also a beginning. Above all, she would try to make her readers see that life always held promise, that there was always another chance for everyone no matter how hopeless things might seem. She began to write it down:

> Today is a new day. You will get out of it just what you put into it. If you have made mistakes, even serious mistakes, there is always another chance for you. And supposing you have tried and failed again and again, you may have a fresh start any moment you choose, for this thing that we call "failure" is not the falling down but the staying down.

I just want to say to one and all—friend and foe alike, "Rejoice not against me, O mine enemy: when I fall, I shall arise; when I sit in darkness, the LORD shall be a light unto me" (Micah 7:8). Let's be clear, the language is correct. It does say, "When I fall," not if. But look at the conclusion of the matter. It goes on to say, "I shall arise!"

This Business of
Living Together

After the death of the famous author, F. Scott Fitzgerald, some-one discovered among his papers a brief statement about an idea for yet another story. It read, "Suggestion for a story—a widely separated family inherits a house in which they all have to live together." It was only a sentence embodying an idea that Fitzgerald was never able to develop. But what if he had? What a potential best seller! "A widely separated family inherits a house in which they all have to live together." We know families in which that experiment would prove interesting, exciting, humorous, dangerous, and ghastly!

Of course, the idea was not original with Fitzgerald. God first had that idea, and he had it a long time ago. Man inherited from God a house—the world—and God said in effect, "Here is your inheritance. It is a big house. The requirement is that you live in it together. I want you to live together in peace and harmony, in love and brotherhood, in kindness and helpfulness. I want you to live together, blessing and being blessed. I want you to live together as a family should live.

"Now you may not choose to live that way. You can partition off the house, put up No Trespassing signs, get guards, watchmen, spies, and armies to protect your own national and personal interests. You can start rumors about each other. You can call each other names and colors. You can harbor all kinds of suspicions and phobias. You can put up your iron, silk, and bamboo curtains, maneuver your spheres of influence and your balances of power, jockey for seats at the United Nations, engage in cold and hot wars. All this you can do if you insist. But I remind you that you are a widely separated family and that you have inherited a house in which you all have to live together. These are the terms of the bequest. Take it together, or leave it together. There is no other earthly house available for you."

We are a family. God's Word declares it. He has made all nations one. He created each, and all are made in His image. We are a family. Science proclaims it. Science is as emphatic about this basic unity as is Genesis. We are a family. History records it. History is "His Story," and the record is legible for all who will take the time to read of the relationship. We are a family. Experience teaches it. Natural man is about the same the world over and, for the most part, has been unchanged from age to age. Oh, there are trappings of education, culture, and environment that make us seem to differ but strip man of these, and it is easy to see that we are a family.

But we are a widely separated family, not so much by distance anymore—in that regard we live next door to each other—but in ideas, ideals, mores, color, creed, inheritance, and evaluation. Think of it! Russian and American, Jew and Arab, Britain and Egyptian, Dutch and Indonesian, white man, black man, yellow man, brown man, red man, Oriental and Occidental, Christian and non-Christian, believer and nonbeliever—we are a widely separated family. And it is later than we think. How can we be made to see that the moment of man's accounting before the court of inquiry for the brotherhood of man is upon us? For we must all appear before the judgment seat of Christ.

It seems I heard that first on the docket is the case of Cain vs. God regarding the question: "Am I my brother's keeper?"

Killing the Eagle

There is a fable told of two eagles, one of which could outfly the other. The eagle who could not fly quite as high became very jealous and determined to destroy his competitor. Upon meeting a hunter, he said, "I wish you would bring that eagle down."

"Well," replied the hunter, "I believe I could do that if I just had some feathers to put into the arrow."

The eagle immediately pulled a feather from his own wing for the hunter's arrow. As the hunter pulled the bowstring, the eagle sat in eager anticipation. The rival eagle, however, was flying so high that the arrow could not quite reach him. Burning with envy at the fantastic display of strength of the other bird, the eagle pulled out more feathers for the hunter's arrows. After each near miss of the target, the envious eagle quickly plucked out more of his plumage until he couldn't fly at all; and the hunter turned and killed him.

I feel that each man who ever lived has at some time in his life experienced the twinge of envy upon seeing someone with an accomplishment or a possession he would like to call his own. But even though this is common to all men, the nurturing of envy can bring only destruction and heartache. The Christian is admonished to "prefer your brother," "do unto others as you would have them do unto you," and "love your neighbor as yourself." The first recorded murder in the Bible was caused by jealousy. And Lucifer was cast out of heaven because he wanted to ascend above the throne of God.

"There will always be someone willing to hurt you, put you down, gossip about you, belittle your accomplishments, and judge your soul. It is a fact that we all must face. However, if you realize that God is a best friend that stands beside you when others cast stones, you will never be afraid, never feel worthless and never feel alone." "I am convinced that the jealous, the angry, the bitter, and the egotistical are the first to race to the top of mountains. A confident person enjoys the journey, the people they meet along the way, and sees life not as a competition.

Proverbs 14:30 says, "A heart at peace gives life to the body, but envy rots the bones." And Eliphaz spake from the pulpit of Brother Job and said, "Surely, resentment destroys the fool, and jealousy kills the simple." And in the sweetheart's chapter of the New Testament, 1 Corinthian 13:4, Paul wrote, "Love is patient, love is kind. It [love] does not envy, it does not boast, it is not proud."

It has been said, and I quote, "Jealousy is a strong emotion that can break any strong relationship. Anger, resentment, and jealousy don't change the heart of others—it only changes yours. Love looks through a telescope; envy, through a microscope."—Author Unknown

Envy handed me my assignment and pointed me to a microscope. But love knew my need best and handed me a telescope. Through it, I saw in the distant past the heart of my Savior filled with love for me on an old rugged cross at Calvary.

On the Hillside of Prayer

They that sow in tears shall reap in joy. He that goeth forth and weepeth, bearing precious seed, shall doubtless come again with rejoicing...

—Psalm 126:5–6

But this I say, He which soweth sparingly shall reap also sparingly; and he which soweth bountifully shall reap also bountifully.

—2 Corinthians 9:6

Jean Giono tells the story of Elzeard Bouffier, a shepherd he met in 1913 in the French Alps. At that time, because of careless deforestation, the mountains around Provence, France, were barren. Former villages were deserted because their springs and brooks had run dry. The wind blew furiously, unimpeded by foliage. While mountain climbing, Giono came to a shepherd's hut where he was invited to spend the night. After dinner, Giono watched the shepherd meticulously sort through a pile of acorns, discarding those that were cracked or undersized. When the shepherd had counted out one hundred perfect acorns, he stopped for the night and went to bed.

Giono learned that the fifty-five-year-old shepherd had been planting trees on the wild hillsides for over three years. He had planted one hundred thousand trees, twenty thousand of which had sprouted. Of those, he expected half to be eaten by rodents or die due to the elements and the other half to live.

After World War I, Giono returned to the mountainside and discovered incredible rehabilitation. There was a veritable forest accompanied by a chain reaction in nature. Water flowed in the once empty brooks. The ecology, sheltered by a leafy roof and bonded to the earth by a mat of spreading roots, became hospitable. Willows, rushes, meadows, gardens, and flowers were birthed.

Giono returned again after World War II. Twenty miles from the lines, the shepherd had continued his work, ignoring the war of 1939, just as he had ignored that of 1914. The reformation of the land continued. Whole regions glowed with health and prosperity. His story of the shepherd's work continues: "On the site of the ruins I had seen in 1913 now stood neat farms. The old streams, fed by the rains and snows that the forest conserved, were flowing again. Little by little, the villages had been rebuilt. People from the plains, where land is costly, had settled here, bringing youth, motion, the spirit of adventure."

There is a hard-to-be-explained feeling of seeing a return on investment—of having planted seed out of sight of the eyes of the unknowing, uncaring—when one prays. Those who pray are like spiritual reforesters, digging holes in barren land and planting the seeds of life. Through these seeds, dry spiritual wastelands are transformed into harvestable fields, and life-giving water is brought to parched and barren souls.

I suppose that only heaven will know the blessing, the benefit, the souls rescued, the help given just in the moment of need all because someone planted a seed on a hillside of prayer. In fact, without doubt, when you plant seeds of prayer, they are never "gone and forgotten." The giver of life also gives life to the seeds of prayer. And there will be evidence of the planting one day.

> Cast thy bread upon the waters: for thou shalt
> find it after many days. (Ecclesiastes 11:1)

One Man Risked Everything

For when we were yet without strength, in due time Christ died for the ungodly. For scarcely for a righteous man will one die: yet peradventure for a good man some would even dare to die. But God commendeth his love toward us, in that, while we were yet sinners, Christ died for us. Much more then, being now justified by his blood, we shall be saved from wrath through him. For if, when we were enemies, we were reconciled to God by the death of his Son, much more, being reconciled, we shall be saved by his life.

—Romans 5:6–10

Battlefields and war join to create strange and heartwarming stories. Such is the subject for our consideration today. Come take a journey with me to the front lines in Europe. As often happens in the fighting of our battles, the exact location sometimes is not known.

It was 1944, and Bert Frizen, who was an infantryman in the American forces, had advanced with his patrol in the face of intermittent shelling throughout the morning hours. But now, all was quiet. His patrol reached the edge of a wooded area with an open field before them. Unknown to the Americans, a battery of Germans was ready and waiting in a hedgerow about two hundred yards across the field.

Bert was one of the two scouts who moved out into the clearing. Once he was halfway across the field, the remainder of his battalion followed. Suddenly, the Germans opened fire and machine gun fire ripped into both of Bert's legs. The American battalion withdrew into the woods for protection, while a rapid exchange of fire continued.

Bert lay helplessly in a small stream as shots volleyed overhead from side to side. There seemed to be no way out of his dilemma. To make matters worse, he now noticed that a German soldier was crawling toward him. Death appeared imminent. He closed his eyes and waited. To his surprise, a considerable period of time passed without the expected attack; so he ventured, opening his eyes again. He was startled to see the German kneeling at his side, smiling. He also noticed that the shooting had stopped. Troops from both sides of the battlefield watched anxiously. Without any verbal exchange, this mysterious German reached down to lift Bert in his strong arms and proceeded to carry him to the safety of his own American comrades.

Having accomplished his self-appointed mission and still without speaking a word, the German soldier turned and walked back across the field to his own troop. No one dared break the silence of this sacred moment. Moments later, the cease-fire ended, but not before all those present had witnessed the power of self-sacrificing love—how one man risked everything for his enemy.

Bert's life was saved through the compassion of one man—his enemy. This courageous act pictures what Jesus has done for us: "While we were still God's enemies, Christ died for us" (Romans 5:8).

Open your eyes, my friend. He is not your enemy but your Savior!

Who Do You Go To?

Stories for the Heart, compiled by Alice Gray, published in 1996 by Vision House Publishing Inc., tells of a young man whose father experienced something very unusual while he was deer hunting in the forests of Oregon.

Cradling his rifle in the crook of his arm, his dad was following an old logging road nearly overgrown by the encroaching forest. It was early evening, and he was just thinking about returning to camp when a noise exploded in the brush nearby. Before he even had a chance to lift his rifle, a small blur of brown and white came shooting up the road straight for him.

The young man laughs as he tells the story.

> It all happened so fast; Dad hardly had time to think. He looked down, and there was a little brown cottontail—utterly spent—crowded up against his legs between his boots. The little thing was trembling all over, but it just sat there and didn't budge. Now this was strange. Wild rabbits are frightened of people, and it's not that often you'd ever actually see one—let alone have one come and sit at your feet.
>
> While Dad was puzzling over this, another player entered the scene. Down the road—maybe twenty yards away—a weasel burst out of the brush. When it saw my dad—and its intended prey sitting at his feet—the predator froze in its tracks, its mouth panting, its eyes glowing red. It was then that Dad understood he had stepped

into a little life-and-death drama of the forest. The cottontail, exhausted by the chase, was only moments from death. Dad was its last hope of refuge. Forgetting its natural fear and caution, the little animal instinctively crowded up against him for protection from the sharp teeth of its relentless enemy. The young man's father did not disappoint. He raised his powerful rifle and deliberately shot into the ground just underneath the weasel. The animal seemed to leap almost straight into the air a couple of feet and then rocketed back into the forest as fast as it could move.

For a while, the little rabbit didn't stir. It just sat there, huddled at the man's feet in the gathering twilight while he spoke gently to it. "Where did it go, little one? I don't think he'll be bothering you for a while. Looks like you're off the hook tonight." Soon the rabbit hopped away from its protector into the forest.

Where, precious friends, do you run in time of need? Where do you run when the predators of trouble, worry, and fear pursue you? Where do you hide when your past pursues you like a relentless wolf, seeking your destruction? Where do you seek protection when the weasels of temptation, corruption, and evil threaten to overtake you? Where do you turn when your energy is spent, when weakness saps you and you feel you cannot run away any longer? Do you turn to your protector, the One who stands with arms open wide, waiting for you to come and huddle in the security of all He is? May I offer a suggestion? There is a friend that sticks closer than a brother, and he said, "Come unto me, and I will give you rest."

It's Gonna Rain!

As the drought continued for what seemed an eternity, a small community of Midwestern farmers were in a quandary as to what to do. The rain was important, not only to keep the crops healthy but to sustain the townspeople's very way of living. As the problem became more urgent, the local church felt it was time to get involved and planned a prayer meeting to ask for rain.

On the agreed upon day and time, the people began to show. The Pastor soon arrived and watched as his congregation continued to file in. He slowly circulated from group to group as he made his way to the front to officially begin the meeting. Everyone he encountered was visiting across the aisles, enjoying the chance to socialize with their close friends. As the Pastor finally secured his place in front of his flock, his thoughts were on the importance of this meeting. He wanted to open the meeting in the best way possible.

Just as he began asking for quiet, he noticed an elevenyear-old girl sitting in the front row. She was angelically beaming with excitement, and lying next to her was her bright red umbrella, poised for use. The beauty and innocence of this sight made the Pastor smile to himself as he realized the faith this young girl possessed that the rest of the people in the room seemed to have forgotten. For a while, the rest had come just to pray for rain; she had come to see God answer.

So virtually clutch your red umbrella that you wish you had brought to the meeting, and hear the words of our dear brother and apostle, James. "My friends," he begins, "what good is it for one of you to say that you have faith if your actions do not prove it? Can that faith save you? Suppose there are brothers or sisters who need clothes and don't have enough to eat, what good is there in your saying to them, "God bless you! Keep warm and eat well!" if you don't give them the necessities of life? So it is with faith: if it is alone and includes no actions, then it is dead" (James 2:14–17 GNB).

If I were present in that praying-for-rain church group, and if James was speaking, then I'd be squirming in regret for having left my umbrella at home. Listen; James is continuing: "You see, then, that it is by our actions that we are put right with God and not by our faith alone. It was the same with the prostitute Rahab [at Jericho]. She was put right with God through her actions by welcoming the Israelite spies and helping them to escape by a different road. So then, as the body without the spirit is dead, also faith without actions is dead" (James 2:24–26 GNB).

My friend Jack Leaman has written much about faith. The title of one of his books speaks to the subject at hand with such clarity: *Faith Brings an Empty Basket* or a red umbrella to a praying-for-rain prayer meeting. And because actions speak louder than words, I, for one, am determined to find my umbrella and keep it handy; for there is a sound of abundance of rain.

Don't forget your galoshes, too!

The Bridge Builder

Lay aside your simple thoughts and leave your paths behind. Agree with my (wisdom's) ways, live in my truth, and righteousness you will find.

—Proverbs 9:6 (TPT)

If you want to live, give up your foolishness and let understanding guide your steps.

—Proverbs 9:6 (CEV)

None should attempt to go through life without consideration of the journey ahead. And having traveled a bit toward the horizon, neither should one fail to cast a glance behind to consider their footprints left on the path. Not that you shall return this way again, but rather, someone may be following the steps you have made, using them as their guide. Leave a trail of white pebbles of goodness dropped along the path like Hansel and Gretel did in *Grimms' Fairy Tales*. Unlike the story told by the Grimm brothers, life is not a fairy tale, its' the real deal.

There will be others following your steps. Therefore, consider well the responsibility that is upon your shoulders to leave footsteps—a well-marked path to be followed—leading them as the Lord leads you. You remember, do you not, David's own words in the shepherd's psalm? "He leadeth me in the paths of righteousness for his name's sake." Be it to everlasting life or to eternal damnation, the path chosen by you will also be trodden by others. This poem speaks of each generation's responsibilities to its successors:

The Bridge Builder

An old man, going a lone highway,
Came, at the evening, cold and gray,
To a chasm, vast, and deep, and wide,
Through which was flowing a sullen tide.
The old man crossed in the twilight dim;
The sullen stream had no fears for him;
But he turned, when safe on the other side,
And built a bridge to span the tide.

"Old man," said a fellow pilgrim, near,
"You are wasting strength with building here;
Your journey will end with the ending day;
You never again must pass this way;
You have crossed the chasm, deep and wide
Why build you the bridge at the eventide?"

The builder lifted his old gray head:
"Good friend, in the path I have come," he said,
"There followeth after me today
A youth, whose feet must pass this way.
This chasm, that has been naught to me,
To that fair-haired youth may a pitfall be.
He, too, must cross in the twilight dim;
Good friend, I am building the bridge for him."

—Will Allen Dromgoole

The Camel's Nose

Sometimes, trouble comes looking for us. This tale gives us some advice about how to keep trouble at bay. One cold night, as a sheikh lay in his tent, a camel thrust the flap aside and looked in. "I pray thee, Master," he said, "let me put my nose within the tent, for it is cold outside."

"By all means," yawned the sheikh who was bored and listless from having lain on his pillows all day. "Do so if you wish."

The camel poked his nose into the tent. "If I might but warm my neck also," he said presently.

"It's all the same to me," answered the sheikh.

So the beast stuck his neck inside and contented itself for a while by looking about.

Soon, the camel, who had been turning his head from side to side, spoke up again, "It will take but little more room if I put my forelegs within the tent. I would feel a great deal better."

The sheikh simply shrugged and rolled to one side to make a little more room.

The camel had hardly planted his forefeet within the tent when he said, "Master, I'm keeping the flap open by standing here like this. I think I ought to come all the way inside."

"Whatever you like," the sheikh nodded, moving over some more so the beast might enter.

So the camel came forward and crowded into the tent. No sooner was he inside, then he looked hard at the sheikh. "I think," he said, "that there is not enough room for both of us here. It will be best for you to stand outside as you are the smaller. Then there will be room enough for me."

And with that he pushed the sheikh out into the cold and darkness.

It is a wise rule to resist the beginnings of evil. Paul talks straight to us when he said, "Don't let evil get the best of you; get the best of evil by doing good" (Romans 12:21 MSG). However, in this case, doing good to the camel—i.e., letting the camel put his nose in the tent—is not wise. We are warned in the first portion of the same verse of the KJV, "Be not overcome of evil." And in 2 Thessalonians 3:2, Paul left a prayer request with the Thessalonians, saying, "Pray that we may be kept safe from worthless and evil people. After all, not everyone has faith."—translation: "not everyone who says they believe is a believer."

One last thought on the subject of camels claiming to have a cold nose: We are instructed to be "wise as a serpent but harmless as a dove." The writer to the Hebrews stated that we are to "have [our] senses exercised to discern both good and evil" (Hebrews 5:14).

And by the way, saints, whoever heard of talking camels!

Make It a Million

It was 1942; three men had spent months prospecting for diamonds in a Venezuelan watercourse. They had worked stooping, gathering pebbles, wishing, and hoping for one sign of a diamond. Their clothes were ragged, their sombreros tattered; but they had never thought seriously of quitting until Solano said, "I'm through." Discouraged, physically exhausted, Rafael Solano sat on a boulder in the dry riverbed and made his announcement to his two companions. "I'm through," he said. "There's no use going on any longer. See this pebble? It makes about 999,999 I've picked up and not a diamond so far. If I pick up another, it will be one million. But what's the use? I'm quitting."

Glumly, one of them said, "Pick up another and make it a million."

A magazine ran this unverified story, which the author claims to be true.

"All right," Solano said and stooped, put his hand on a pile of pebbles, and picked one up. It was almost the size of a hen's egg. "Here it is," he said, "the last one." But it was heavy—too heavy. He looked. "Boys, it's a diamond!" he shouted.

Harry Winston, a New York jewel dealer, paid Rafael Solano $200,000 for that millionth pebble. Named the Liberator, it was the largest and purest diamond ever found at that time, weighing in at 155 carats, uncut.

Perhaps Rafael Solano needed no other reward, but I think he must have known a happiness that went beyond the financial. He had set his course. The odds were against him. He had persevered. He had won. He had not only done what he had set out to do—

which was a reward in itself—but he had done it in the face of failure and obscurity.

An old proverb teaches us that half the failures in life come from "pulling in the horse in the midst of his leap." Elihu Root once said, "Men don't fail. They give up trying." Often, it is not the wrong start but the wrong stop that makes the difference between success and failure. To quit while we're ahead would be silly; to quit when we're behind is even sillier. It requires will to hold on a little longer. It requires wit to know that the measure of success is not the luck nor the breaks of the game but the victory over failure. "The trouble with most of us," it has been said, "is that we stop trying in trying times."

A disturbed patient conceded, after several sessions with his psychiatrist, "It's easier to lie on a couch digging into the past than it is to sit on a chair facing the present." It is even harder to get up and walk toward the future. Preoccupation with the past is always a retreat. An old joke makes the point: Two hunters on a safari cornered a lion, who, instead of attacking, turned tail and disappeared into the underbrush. One terrified hunter stammered to the other, "You go ahead and see where he went to. I'll go back and see where he came from."

We often react like that hunter. Tomorrow's problems are unknown; they may cause new pain. Yesterdays are over with; they are still painful. But the pain is familiar, almost comfortable. It is easier, less risky, to take what comfort we can out of our accustomed miseries. And sooner or later, we find ourselves incapable of moving forward; we are trapped in the quicksand of our own regrets. David Livingstone, the great explorer, once explained, "I will go anywhere so long as it is forward." Our motivation should be forward; our instincts should be for advancement. Remember, life is growth; and in ceasing to grow, we deny life.

Taking Satan's Lure

Have you heard this before: "I have a talent for making a mess of things"?

Over the years, I've wondered why it is that some people seem to have a talent for finding themselves in "yet another" sad and sorrowful situation filled with sin and shame. They seem to have a propensity for failing.

Propensity—now there is the key. "Propensity implies a deeply ingrained and usually irresistible inclination." An example in a sentence can be, "She has a great propensity for chocolate; therefore, she avoids walking down the candy aisle when shopping."

Not being a fisherman, I write only from what I have read about and heard from some of you. Obviously, the fisherman tries a variety of artificial lures to catch certain species. That's why he carries such a large tackle box because of all the lures he's got. Some days, the fish strike one lure; some days, another. But occasionally, in certain locations, there is one lure that they go for every time. They can't resist it. In fishermen's lingo, "That lure is my touchdown, baby!" (Football?) "Yes, sir, I can hit a home run with that puppy every time!" (Baseball?) (Puppy?) Whew! I need to go back to school just to learn the language. Holding their home-run lure, they will show where it has been chewed so many times by fish fighting to dislodge the hook. These fishermen know the fish they're after have a weakness, and they know what it is. Because they know, they can catch them.

Satan knows the weakness of every one of us too. He has a lot of different lures to dangle in front of us, and he's not shy about using them. But for each of us, he has a favorite lure. He knows we can't resist.

Occasionally, a fish will pull loose, ripping its skin; and with mouth hanging down, it goes off to heal. But the scars will always be there. Sometimes, we can pull away from Satan too but not before some painful tearing occurs, causing scars that will remain for the rest of our lives. For even when we are made whole again by receiving and accepting forgiveness, the physical and sometimes the emotional results of what we did won't go away. Christians get emotionally, physically, and spiritually hurt, and they hurt others too.

There are so many painful ways for the people of God to stumble, and Satan knows every one of them. He's got a tackle box full of lures. As he studies believers, he knows he probably can't make us denounce the Lord, but he can tempt us into a compromise with sin. Satan knows exactly how to make each one of us fall. Our weaknesses are no secret to him.

Knowing what we are like and how our minds work, Satan will aim where we are vulnerable. A person may not be tempted with greed but might be tempted with the pride that grows out of not being greedy. The person who can't stand the taste of liquor will probably not become an alcoholic but might be battling an addiction to pornography. Satan knows how to get to our weak spots. He knows where they are.

Three things are certain about messing up our lives: First, we don't have to yield to temptation. God has made a way of escape. Second, if we do slip, we don't have to wallow in our mistakes. There is deliverance. Third, we can use the lesson learned from falling, not only to avoid falling again but to help some other person who is facing similar pressures.

So remember, if you have a propensity for chocolate, don't go near that aisle.

The Slippery Slope

Stress, probably more than any other factor, determines the point at which we find ourselves on the slide down the slippery slope from health to illness. Stress is not unique to our own country or time, but given our way of living, we can accurately label it a "North American disease." Let's look at our national background to see why this is so.

One factor is the urge to achieve. At a recent symposium, one of the questions discussed by a panel attempting to reassess the current values of society and culture was, "Why do we have such a strong impulse to get ahead?" One conclusion was that the Quakers and Puritans who talked about salvation by faith nevertheless behaved as though temporal works were ultimately the true measure of heavenly achievement. These early settlers worked hard, were ambitious, and frugal. And many prospered.

The typical mindset of those who came to the New World hoped to do good by doing well. They had the drive to get ahead. If they did not already have the drive, society motivated them to get it. Idleness was considered a sin and sometimes even a crime. Benjamin Franklin helped establish laziness as a vice in the national consciousness.

Drive led men to hack their way through a wilderness caused women like Jane Addams to minister tirelessly to the slum dwellers in Chicago, led the Wright brothers to prove that man can fly, and moved Jonas Salk to conquer polio. Individuals such as Henry Ford put the automobile within the reach of nearly everyone's pocketbook. And who hasn't been grateful on a hot and humid summer day for Willis H. Carrier when the announcement was published on the sign attached to a building, "Refrigeration cooled."

Sometimes, we can't forget the push that feels almost tangible. It blares at us constantly on radio and social media. It is plastered on subway billboards. We hear it in the marketplace. "Do you want to get ahead?" As a result of the push, with due consideration for all the benefits it has brought us, stress has become a way of life. Dr. Eugene Jennings, management consultant and adviser to executives, has pointed out that people suffer from energy fatigue.

We might be tempted to say complacently, "Well, I'm glad I'm not caught up in such a competitive rat race." But we are all subject to the ravages of stress. We would like to think that stress affects others only, but such an assumption is false.

There is a story of European missionaries serving in Africa a century ago. They hired local villagers as porters to help carry supplies to a distant station several days' journey away. The porters went at a slower pace than the missionaries desired; so after the first two days, they pushed them to go faster. On day 3 of the trek, the group went twice as far as day 2. Around the campfire that evening, the missionaries congratulated themselves for their leadership abilities. But on day 4, the workers would not budge.

"What's wrong?" asked the missionary.

"We cannot go any further today," replied the villagers' spokesman.

"Why not? Everyone appears well."

"Yes," said the African, "but we went so quickly yesterday that we must wait here for our souls to catch up with us."

Be honest with yourself now, have you been pushing your life a little too hard? Is it time to let your soul catch up? Jesus said, "Come unto me, and I will give you rest."

Just Outside the Door

When the snow lies deep in the North, when the cold of forty and fifty below strikes through to the bone, a roaring fire is most comfortable and welcome. Yet there are always men who are duty bound to venture forth on the coldest days and nights, fulfilling their tasks as only the men of the North can; and Victor Clarke, president of the Clarke Advertising Service of Victoria, BC, was one who was in this position while serving as broker for the Hudson's Bay Company post at Fort Babine.

Although the weather was very heavy and cold, Mr. Clarke, with a young Indian as his companion, left the comforts of Fort Babine and journeyed to Hazelton for supplies. All went well on the journey. They reached Hazelton safely. Mr. Clarke obtained his supplies, exchanged news and pleasantries with those who served them, and began the homeward trek across the snow-covered wastes of the North.

While they were mushing along the homeward trail, snow began to fall, soon increasing in volume. A stinging wind cut the faces of the two men on the trail. The newly fallen snow slogged on their snowshoes and impeded their progress. The driving wind, increasing with every passing mile, whipped their faces and chilled them to the bone. Colder and colder, they became. Faster and faster, fell the snow. Although the winter gale was increasingly more ferocious, these winter travelers were determined to make it to Fort Babine before night engulfed them. But darkness descended upon them, and they could keep to the trail only with great difficulty. They began to feel faint and to stumble in the heavy snow of the trail. Then Clarke turned to his Indian companion and asked, "How much farther is it to Fort Babine?"

The Indian, after pausing for a moment, said, "Ten miles."

Reluctantly, Mr. Clarke decided to camp beneath a clump of trees. There they passed a terrible night. They built a small campfire. But weary with hunger and cold and with the wind whistling through the trees, chilling them to the bone, they could only hope for the day. Meanwhile, the snowfall became deeper and deeper with the passing hours. Then the gray dawn began to appear, ushering in another day. They had spent a tortuous night and were glad to see the dawn break over the winter wilderness.

"Look!" Mr. Clarke cried, pointing off in the distance. They stood amazed! They had camped, hungry and cold, during the hours of darkness, within a few hundred yards of the comforts of Fort Babine! They had camped just outside the door! And they did not know it!

This story reminds me of an experience my father had while serving as manager of custodial maintenance at the little twelve-bed Sierra View Hospital in Visalia, California. Going to work at 4:00 a.m. as was his routine, he began his "security walk-through" from the front entrance all the way to the back entrance. At the backdoor, he had difficulty opening the door. Using some force, he managed to push the door open, only to find a young woman deceased—frozen in a standing position—leaning against the door. Apparently seeking help during the night, she made it to the door but did not get in!

My friends, are you camping just outside the door of hope, peace, and rest that is found in Christ? Do you realize that you are camping just outside the door of salvation? You no longer need to camp in sin's dark night, with the cold winds of the world chilling you to the bone, just outside the door of salvation. Jesus Christ will bring you in to the warmth and protection of His presence. Jesus said, "I am the door: by me if any man enter in, he shall be saved." Unlike the lady whom my father found, if you will knock, even ever so faintly, He will hear you and open the door to you."

Say It!

O give thanks unto the LORD, for he is good: for his mercy endureth forever. Let the redeemed of the LORD say so, whom he hath redeemed from the hand of the enemy;

—Psalm 107:1–2

Reverend Bernard Washington Spilman, a clergyman and denominational Sunday School executive, wrote the following article, which would lighten many loads and brighten many hearts if put into practice. He wrote:

You have a friend—a man, a woman, a boy or a girl. For some reason you love him very much. Have you ever told him so? Perhaps he would like to have you say it. Your friend has helped you along the way in the days gone by. Gratitude is in your heart. Do not let it lie buried there—say it.

Some joy has come his way. You rejoice with him. But he will never know it unless you say it. An honor comes to him. He wins in the game of life, and you are glad—say it. Your friend succeeds in some tasks which he has undertaken. You feel a grateful pride that he has done it—say it.

A sorrow comes his way. He may have lost his property. Some of his loved ones may have gone wrong. Disease may have laid its hand on him, taking away the glow of health. You would share the sorrow with him—say it.

Old age, or perhaps a breakdown in the human machinery [of his body], may shut in your friend so that he can no longer go forth among his fellows. Perhaps the end draws near. In your heart you wish him bon voyage as he nears the sunset gate. A word of kindly sympathy would brighten the way—say it.

The messenger of death may have knocked at his door and borne away into the unseen world some loved one. A word of sympathy would help to lighten the load and brighten the way—say it.

A personal word, a telephone call, a postcard, a letter, a telegram, and only a few minutes of time! Silent sympathy. Your own life may be better because of it; but your friend may go to the end of the journey and never know. You may add to the joy; You may lighten the load; You may brighten the way if you only take time to—say it.

As I'm putting Spilman's article into this devotion, the weight of his message is pressing me with deep conviction, causing myself to cast my mind to consider those whom I shall communicate with. Surely, we all find ourselves in similar struggles of consciousness from time to time. Some of the struggles are, of course, guilt, shame for the neglect, the curse of busyness, the awkwardness because of the passage of time—so many reasons why we haven't "kept up." But really, we need to buck up, square our shoulders, and just do it.

But to do good and to communicate forget not: for with such sacrifices God is well pleased. (Hebrews 13:16)

Rubber Boots, Irrigation Ditches, and Things that Cling

Mr. Sarquis owned 80 acres of fruit orchards and 160 acres of cotton fields in the fertile San Joaquin Valley of California. He was my father's employer for almost fifteen years. As a small child, during the summertime, I would go to the orchards with Dad. While he worked, I would build forts out of the large wooden field lugs (boxes) that were used to transport the peaches and plums to the packing shed. That was always a lot of fun, especially since there was plenty of nice fresh fruit to be eaten.

As I grew a bit older, Dad used to take me with him to "set pipe." Now, if you have never participated in "changing the water" on a cotton farm, you have missed out on some very interesting (and hard) work. Dad would let me ride the old, gray Ford-Ferguson tractor with the big V-shaped "ditching" plow attached to the three-point hitch. With great effort, a channel would be made to carry water along the end of the field perpendicular to the rows of cotton. When completed, the ditch would run from the pump pool to the end of the field. Then Dad would throw the switch on the big ten-inch turbine pump; and with a loud whine of the electric motor amid gurgling sounds coming up out of the well, a beautiful stream of cold, clear water would gush out into the large catching pool to which the ditch was connected. As the water level rose in the pool and then began to flow out into the ditch, we would hastily make our way to the end of that day's "setting" where Dad had placed the dam.

The purpose of setting the dam was to stop up the ditch with a large sheet of metal shaped in a half circle. About five feet in diameter, it was stiffened across the top with a piece of pipe welded along the spine. It was awesome to watch my Dad raise that huge piece of metal into the air and slam it down across the ditch, effectively creating a dam. This would force the water level in the ditch to rise sufficient for setting pipe. These were lightweight aluminum pipes about one and a half inches in diameter by four feet long. Shaped like a question mark, these pipes were curved in a half circle and bent at the end so as to go up over the edge of the ditch and lie flat in the furrow. By putting one end in the water and sluicing it up and down with the hand, alternately closing and opening over the other end of the pipe, a suction would be created, thus lifting the water from the ditch into the furrows of cotton. With a small stream of water flowing from the pipe, it would be "set" in the furrow and left to run overnight. Although it really was quite effective, setting pipe has become outmoded today, being replaced by large field sprinkling systems. Now, before this turns into a *Farmer's Irrigation Manual*, several observations should be made.

- Our Heavenly Father has rescued us all from slippery places. This should always be the first remembrance in our relationship with God. When irrigating, it was necessary to wear knee-high rubber boots. It was also necessary to stay in them. Unfortunately, a few times, I had the misadventure of stepping in deep mud and succeeding in getting my boot stuck. While attempting to pull my foot out of the mud, my foot came out of the boot, and the boot stayed in the mud. So then the object was to remain upright on one foot while holding the other foot out of the mud so as not to get your sock dirty. More than once, it was Dad that came to my rescue, wrapping his strong arms around me and lifting me, my boots, shovel, and all to higher (I mean drier) ground. Now that I think about it, there's been a few times when the good Lord has wrapped His strong arms around me, rescuing me from some pretty muddy places.

- Rising levels of blessing moves the junk out of our lives. The second observation is this: All the trash and debris in the ditch were carried along on the rising water level until it reached the dam where it gathered in a swirling, foamy glob. The floating leaves and paper, even small wood chips, could stop the flow of water through the siphon tubes. Of necessity, the debris and flotsam had to be scooped out of the ditch so that nothing but pure water was flowing into the furrows. How damaging to our lives and the lives of others when the flow of God's Spirit is obstructed by trash and superficial stuff that tends only to impede the flow of the Holy Ghost. The obstructed flow of the Holy Spirit results in the deprivation in young, tender lives of the life-giving water of the Spirit so badly needed.

- Lay aside every weight of hurtful things clinging to your life. This removal of irritants can be replicated in the spiritual. A forgiving spirit augmented with heartfelt prayer and love for the brethren can go a long way in helping to remove things that cling—those irritants that, after a while, begin to vex the soul. Pettiness, jealousies, hurt feelings, snubs (both real and imagined) are all little foxes that quite often spoil so much of God's goodness in our lives.

The final observation has to do with things that cling. My Dad always had clean fields. He kept the weeds cut down. While standing at the end of the field with Mr. Sarquis or George Shuklian or one of the several farmers stopping by to trade crop talk, Dad was never idle. He would constantly be chopping weeds, bending over to pluck up by the roots some large noxious weed, or digging up the roots of grass, trying to spread through the field. It was this involvement with persistence that kept his fields clean but at a price. For when we would stop under the big, old poplar tree for lunch, I noticed something. Dad always pulled off his boots. Then he would pick off the stickers, the foxtails, the cockle-burrs, and such that were clinging to his socks. Thus, in the middle of the day, he removed a lot of small irritations.

In His marvelous wisdom, our Heavenly Father has picked us up out of some very sticky places. And with the rising level of His benediction upon our lives, He has bidden us to have lunch with Him under the old poplar tree to settle down, take off our boots, and pick out the little things that cling. If we will do this—when we learn to do this—the rest of the day's work will be so much more pleasant.

Incognito!

Waiting in line outside the bank, I was preoccupied with my admittedly negative thoughts. *This is crazy. Whoever heard of having to wait outside of a bank before you could go in to transact business! People get arrested for hanging around outside banks! I just wanted to make a deposit for one of my elderly church members.* Grumble, grumble, grum—

"Hi, Mr. Mason!"

I gazed without recognizing the one speaking to me from behind his face mask and then realized it was one of the officers of the bank. Good thing I had my mask on, or he might have seen the grumbling expression on my face.

I have become more aware of the masks worn by different people in our multicultural community. More to the point, I've begun looking at their eyes. Before it was always said that "she has a nice smile," or "his expression was very stern. He didn't even smile." Now, if you want to share a smile, it must come from your eyes, the "window of the soul." One of the cashiers at our grocery store always has a nice, happy smile. She is pleasant. And when we can, often my wife and I choose her checkout lane for her joyful attitude. I have noticed in these "post-mask days" that her smile is still firmly in place because I can see it in her eyes!

Your eyes reveal your true self. They are the windows of the soul. Since the advent of wearing masks as part of our daily routine, Gloria has been concerned that "it just makes it easier for people to commit crimes. You know, they can rob the bank much easier now because everyone is wearing a mask." Of course I contend; if you have larceny in your heart, a mask won't make a difference. You'll rob anyhow. (I feel a sermon coming on.) It's not what's behind your mask; it's what's in your heart.

What's behind your mask?—unhappiness, discontent, anger, yes, grumbling. We must remember the window of the soul. The eyes have it. They show it. So if your smile got tipped over, you may need to do a little attitude repair and turn your frown upside down! There. That's better. Your eyes are letting in the light that brightens the day.

I found a lady's mask in my driveway this week. Someone lost her mask. Quite a nice one too. So now, there is a lady who is going to be seen at *face* value. She has nothing to hide behind. This is not the new normal; rather it is the old original. God made us all with our *faces* in full view. Therefore, we must not think the mask hides anything. When Sarai became heavy-handed, Hagar fled from Sarai's *face*. She couldn't *face* her anymore. And when Moses was in the presence of God on the mountain, his *face* shined with the glory of God so much so that he had to cover his *face* with a veil for the people's sake!

And so, pandemic-surviving, face-mask-wearing soldiers of the cross, be not weary in hand sanitizing and social distancing. You may not understand it all right now, nor do I. For now, we see through a glass darkly but then face-to-face.

Jesus loves you. You don't have to look in His eyes. Look at the palms of His hands!

Between You and the Sea

Yea, though I walk through the valley of the shadow of death, I will fear no evil: for thou art with me; thy rod and thy staff they comfort me.

—Psalm 23:4

I think the wisest man is the man that is afraid; only fools do not know what fear is. But there must be something that suggests to the mind that there is a superiority over fear. A man needs to take hold of something more than a pure fancy of the mind. This mastery over fear must need to be established upon substance, not mere delusional imagination. This takes faith.

There it was again. A man was in the hallway, just outside my bedroom door. He had just moved his arm. I was as scared as any ten-year-old boy could be. I mean, I was so scared; my voice would not work. I wanted to cry out to Momma, but when I did, my voice would not make a sound. I was frozen in horror! Apparently, I was making noises of some kind, no doubt the whimpering sounds of a fearful child, for Mother heard me and called, "France. What's wrong with you?"

"There's a man outside my bedroom."

I heard Mother getting out of bed (she let my hardworking Dad sleep undisturbed) and made her way into the hallway. "Oh, son, that's not a man. You're just seeing my coat hanging here, and the wind is blowing the sleeve around. Now go back to sleep. Everything is okay."

Whew! What a close call. What comforting words. Now I could breathe again.

There must be something strong enough to draw a man's thoughts away from the dark corner, the cave where the enemy lurks, where the feared shadow appears to be. And there is that something—a strength! For me, as a child, it was Mother's comforting voice. But for all who are traversing through the valley of fear, it is one who has the form of a shepherd, and the substance of a rod and a staff, both well-used in previous conflicts with the enemy. David had faced the enemy of fear while walking through the shadowy valley of death. He was a man, a human just as you; but listen to his antidote for the fearful shadows: "I will fear no evil: for thou art with me."

So look at this twofold encouragement: "Thou art with me" and "Thy rod and thy staff they comfort me." God puts Himself as a shelter and a breakwater (a strong pile of huge rocks) between us and that great sea of danger out there. Its billows are roundabout us in their fearful turmoil. But if I may mix my metaphors, He, the strong and mighty Shepherd of Psalm 23, says, "Get behind me child. Let me be in front of you. I am the breakwater—the sea is calm if you let me stand between you and the storm."

His presence—His unshakeable, never-changing presence—is the only thing that can make you strong. Trust in Him. He alone has the power to remain undefeated and unmoved by the stormy sea. Regardless of the storm, He is there for you—between you and the sea.

I'm trusting in the Rock of Ages. When I look toward the storm, all I can see is Jesus in between.

I Lost It All to Find Everything

I had won all I could win, there was no place I hadn't been.
But my heart was so needy and so poor.
Then I heard Him gently say, "Lose it all, and find my way."
So I gave it up and found it all and more.
I lost it all to find everything, I died a pauper to become a king.
When I learned how to lose, I found out how to win.
Oh, I lost it all to find everything.
I was frantic to survive, I was racing to arrive.
And I walked on any standing in my way.
Then I watched my schemes all die and realized that I
Could find new life, because the old had died that day.

—Sammy Hall

It was way into the night—bedtime and past. The end of a weary and heavy-laden day. I felt to spend a moment with my soul in a worshipful, spiritual environment. So instead of turning off my computer screen, I entered the sanctuary of praise. Now I know the eyebrows of some of you will need retrieving; but you listen to your kind of music, and I'll listen to mine. I heard a song unfamiliar to me, but the title was captivating. As the sounds of the orchestra filled the room, the words and music of Bill and Gloria Gaither began to penetrate the encrusted shell of the days' mental debris.

I lost it all to find everything. I died a pauper to become a king. When I learned how to lose, I found out how to win.

Opposites. The fantastic results of a new life, a new birth. I gave it up and found it all—and more. I died a pauper to become a king. From living (?) in darkness, I saw the light! Surrounded by all the doom and gloom of the old, Jesus brought to me the new. A smile replaced the frown. He lifted me up; no longer was I down. With repentance, down on my knees, I died to sin and shame. After the cleansing plunge of baptism, I arose to walk in the newness of life, speaking a heavenly tongue, leaving cursing and blasphemy in the past. In short, I'm walking a new road now. The destination on the GPS of my life has been changed from the flames of hell to the streets of gold.

I found a new life because the old died the day I met Jesus. And, my friend, it is no secret. What He's done for others, He'll do for you if you want Him to.

Most Richly Blessed

We're a rugged breed, us quads (quadriplegics). If we weren't, we wouldn't be around today. Yes, we're a rugged breed. In many ways, we've been blessed with a savvy and spirit that isn't given to everybody. And let me say that this refusal of total or full acceptance of one's disability all hooks up with one thing—faith, an almost divine faith.

Down in the reception room of the Institute of Physical Medicine and Rehabilitation, over on the East River at 400 East 34th Street in New York City, there's a bronze plaque that's riveted to the wall. During the months of coming back to the Institute for treatment—two or three times a week—I rolled through that reception room many times, coming, and going. But I never quite made the time to pull over to one side and read the words on that plaque that were written by an unknown soldier from the US Civil War.

Then one afternoon, I did. I read it and then I read it again. When I finished it for the second time, I was near to bursting—not in despair, but with an inner glow that had me straining to grip the arms of my wheelchair. I'd like to share it with you.

—Roy Campanella

A Creed for Those Who Have Suffered

I asked God for strength, that I might achieve.
I was made weak, that I might learn humbly to obey.
I asked for health, that I might do great things.
I was given infirmity, that I might do better things.
I asked for riches, that I might be happy.
I was given poverty, that I might be wise.
I asked for power, that I might have the praise of men.
I was given weakness, that I might feel the need of God.
I asked for all things, that I might enjoy life.
I was given life, that I might enjoy all things.
I got nothing I asked for, but everything I had hoped for.
Almost despite myself, my unspoken prayers were answered.
I am, among men, most richly blessed!

—an unknown soldier from the US civil war

Roy Campanella, nicknamed "Campy," was my favorite baseball player in my thirteenth year mostly because he was a really good catcher; and I wanted to be a really good catcher just like him. His playing career ended when he was paralyzed in an automobile accident in January 1958. He is widely considered to be one of the greatest catchers in the history of the game.

> But without faith it is impossible to please him: for he that cometh to God must believe that he is, and that he is a rewarder of them that diligently seek him. (Hebrews 11:6)

The 38th Hour!

Mark V. Hansen tells this miraculous story of the horrible earthquake in Armenia. In 1989, an 8.2 earthquake almost flattened Armenia, killing over thirty thousand people in less than four minutes. Amid utter devastation and chaos, a father left his wife securely at home and rushed to the school where his son was supposed to be, only to discover that the building was as flat as a pancake.

After the traumatic initial shock, he remembered the promise he had made to his son: "No matter what, I'll always be there for you!" And tears began to fill his eyes. As he looked at the pile of debris that once was the school, it looked hopeless, but he kept remembering his commitment to his son.

He began to concentrate on where he walked his son to class at school each morning. Remembering his son's classroom would be in the back right corner of the building. He rushed there and started digging through the rubble.

As he was digging, other forlorn parents arrived, clutching their hearts, saying, "My son!" "My daughter!" Other well-meaning parents tried to pull him from what was left of the school, saying, "It's too late!" "They're dead!" "You can't help!" "Go home!" "Come on. Face reality. There's nothing you can do!" "You're just going to make things worse!"

To each parent, he responded with one line, "Are you going to help me now?" And then he proceeded to dig for his son stone by stone.

The fire chief showed up and tried to pull him from the school's debris, saying, "Fires are breaking out. Explosions are happening everywhere. You're in danger. We'll take care of it. Go home."

To which this loving, caring Armenian father asked, "Are you going to help me now?"

The police came and said, "You're angry, distraught, and it's over. You're endangering others. Go home. We'll handle it!"

To which he replied, "Are you going to help me now?"

No one helped.

Courageously, he proceeded alone because he needed to know for himself: "Is my boy alive, or is he dead?"

He dug for eight hours…twelve hours…twenty-four hours… thirty-six hours. Then, in the thirty-eighth hour, he pulled back a boulder and heard his son's voice.

He screamed his son's name, "*Armand!*"

He heard back, "Dad! It's me, Dad! I told the other kids not to worry. I told 'em that if you were alive, you'd save me. And when you saved me, they'd be saved. You promised, 'No matter what, I'll always be there for you!' You did it, Dad!"

"What's going on in there? How is it?" the father asked.

"There are fourteen of us left out of thirty-three, Dad. We're scared, hungry, thirsty, and thankful you're here. When the building collapsed, it made a wedge, like a triangle. And it saved us."

"Come on out, boy!"

"No, Dad! Let the other kids out first, 'cause I know you'll get me! No matter what, I know you'll be there for me!"

Your heavenly Father made a similar promise to you…and me.

> O Jacob, and O Israel, Fear not: for I have redeemed thee, I have called thee by thy name; thou art mine. When thou passest through the waters, I will be with thee; and through the rivers, they shall not overflow thee: when thou walkest through the fire, thou shalt not be burned; neither shall the flame kindle upon thee. For I am the LORD thy God, the Holy One of Israel, thy Saviour." (Isaiah 43:1–3)

And there is something you can do! Start digging. Our kids are in there somewhere.

Puppies for Sale

And Solomon said, Give therefore thy servant an understanding heart to judge thy people, that I may discern between good and bad: for who is able to judge this thy so great a people? And the speech pleased the Lord, that Solomon had asked this thing. And God said unto him, Because thou hast asked this thing, and hast not asked for thyself long life; neither hast asked riches for thyself, nor hast asked the life of thine enemies; but hast asked for thyself understanding to discern judgment; Behold, I have done according to thy words: lo, I have given thee a wise and an understanding heart.

—1 Kings 3:6, 9–12

A store owner was tacking a sign above his door that read "Puppies For Sale." Signs like that have a way of attracting small children, and sure enough, a little boy appeared under the store owner's sign. "How much are you going to sell the puppies for?" he asked.

The store owner replied, "Anywhere from $30.00 to $50.00."

The little boy reached in his pocket and pulled out some change. "I have $2.37" he said. "Can I please look at them?"

The store owner smiled and whistled and out of the kennel came Lady, who ran down the aisle of his store followed by five teeny, tiny balls of fur. One puppy was lagging considerably behind. Immediately the little boy singled out the lagging, limping puppy and said, "What's wrong with that little dog?"

The store owner explained that the veterinarian had examined the little puppy and had discovered it didn't have a hip socket. It would always limp. It would always be lame. The little boy became excited. "That is the little puppy that I want to buy."

The store owner said, "No, you don't want to buy that little dog. If you really want him, I'll just give him to you."

The little boy got quite upset. He looked straight into the store owner's eyes, pointing his finger, and said, "I don't want you to give him to me. That little dog is worth every bit as much as all the other dogs and I'll pay full price. In fact, I'll give you $2.37 now, and 50 cents a month until I have him paid for."

The store owner countered, "You really don't want to buy this little dog. He is never going to be able to run and jump and play with you like the other puppies."

To this, the little boy reached down and rolled up his pant leg to reveal a badly twisted, crippled left leg supported by a big metal brace. He looked up at the store owner and softly replied, "Well, I don't run so well myself, and the little puppy will need someone who understands!" (Dan Clark in *Weathering the Storm*)

Out of the mouth of babes and sucklings hast thou ordained strength because of thine enemies, that thou mightest still the enemy and the avenger. (Psalm 8:2)

Consider what I say; and the Lord give thee understanding in all things. (2 Timothy 2:7)

Nothing

Let nothing be done through strife or vainglory; but in lowliness of mind let each esteem other better than themselves.

—Philippians 2:3

Be careful for nothing; but in every thing by prayer and supplication with thanksgiving let your requests be made known unto God.

—Philippians 4:6

Every sermon has a subject; after all, when he stands before the people, a preacher has to say something. But today, I am presenting for your consideration: nothing. There are some important "nothings" in the Bible I wish to have you think about this morning.

Perhaps you may think, *Boy, I've seen this one a lot.* But bear with me as we investigate "the 'Nothing' in Christian service." In Philippians 2:3, Paul instructed the saints to "let nothing be done through strife or vain glory." We are not made aware of any specifics regarding strife and/or vain glory among the Philippian church. However, it goes without saying that Satan attempts to trip us up, so to speak, or take us unaware with events or comments made (by us or others) that we did not plan to do or say. For several years, I have on a regular basis made it a part of my prayer to ask God for help in this area. Note the word *let*. It means "to allow." My prayer, on the other hand, places God in charge of events to help me guard against such episodes.

Strife is defined as "bitter, sometimes violent conflict or dissension, an act of contention: a fight or struggle, or exertion or contention for superiority." Any time there is strife in the church, the work of Christ is hindered. There was certainly strife in Corinth. And in Galatians 5, Paul lists strife among the several notoriously bad works of the flesh. And James said, "Strife is earthly, sensual, devilish."

Briefly, allow me to present the "nothing" of anxiety in daily life. The KJV renders Philippians 4:6 to "be careful" for nothing. The modern understanding of this phrase would have us read, "Be anxious for nothing." Unfortunately, we often only obey "be anxious." Therefore, our lives become filled with anxiety, nervousness, and unrest. This can lead to so many unhealthy issues within our bodies, which can destroy our health, homes, dreams, and accomplishments. Anxiety does nothing to help us cope with tomorrow; and it certainly drains strength from today.

Finally, consider the "nothing" of God's Almighty power: "For with God, nothing shall be impossible." Consider the challenge to Mary's faith. She was to give birth to Jesus without having known a man. Every obstacle we face is tempered by this "nothing." Your faith will grow phenomenally by acceptance of this "nothing." As Mary did, accepting Gabriel's "nothing" will chase our doubts away.

I urge all of us to allow "nothing" to hold us back from full commitment to our Lord, Jesus Christ.

Guilty as Charged...or Not!

Blessed is he whose transgression is forgiven, whose sin is covered. Blessed is the man unto whom the LORD imputeth not iniquity, and in whose spirit there is no guile. When I kept silence, my bones waxed old through my roaring all the day long. For day and night thy hand was heavy upon me: my moisture is turned into the drought of summer. Selah. I acknowledged my sin unto thee, and mine iniquity have I not hid. I said, I will confess my transgressions unto the LORD; and thou forgavest the iniquity of my sin. Selah.

—Psalm 32:1–5

Can you identify with a guilty king? He feels miserable and unhappy all day long. What is guilt? "Guilt is the fact or condition of having committed an offense, especially a willful violation of a legal or moral code" (The Reader's Digest Great Encyclopedic Dictionary). This willful violation of moral integrity brings deep feelings of remorse. Let's look at why you feel guilty and what to do about it.

You may feel guilty because you are guilty. David felt guilty because of his sins. So let's admit that we are all guilty before God. Here are some selected statements found in Romans 3:10–25:

As it is written, There is none righteous, no, not one: there is none that doeth good, no, not one. Destruction and misery are in their ways: And

the way of peace have they not known: There
is no fear of God before their eyes. For all have
sinned, and come short of the glory of God.

Like Belshazzar, we've been weighed and found wanting. But
guilt feelings can have a positive effect. They are like the warning
signs of cancer. They are like pains that warn of a serious problem.
They may come from an awakened conscience or from the conviction of the Holy Spirit. However they may come, thank God for guilt
feelings if they bring you to Him.

You may feel guilty because you have not been forgiven. Before
confessing his sins and receiving forgiveness, David felt older than his
years and that God was against him. In our text, he felt as though he
was in a spiritual desert. But forgiveness was available to David, but
he had not accepted it. We have an absolute guarantee of forgiveness
from Almighty God.

If we confess our sins, he is faithful and just to
forgive us our sins, and to cleanse us from all
unrighteousness. (1 John 1:9)

Our forgiveness depends on accepting God's gracious offer to
sinners. Look at it again: "If we confess our sins, he is faithful and
just to forgive us our sins." He is faithful and just. But even grace
does not force forgiveness on us. You can be free from guilt by accepting forgiveness.

Read and identify with the guilty king's confession.

For I acknowledge my transgressions: and my sin
is ever before me. Against thee, thee only, have I
sinned, and done this evil in thy sight: that thou
mightest be justified when thou speakest, and be
clear when thou judgest. (Psalm 51:3–4)

I acknowledged my sin unto thee, and mine iniquity have I not hid. I said, I will confess my trans-

gressions unto the LORD; and thou forgavest the
iniquity of my sin. (Psalm 32:5)

David sought and found forgiveness. David's confession of his
sins fits us all. Sins confessed are sins forgiven. This will always be
true. Why remain a prisoner of past sins? Bring your sins to the one
who died for sinners. You do not have to feel guilty anymore. And
with sins forgiven, "There is therefore now no condemnation to
them which are in Christ Jesus!" (Romans 8:1).

Truth Never Changes!

Buy the truth, and sell it not; also wisdom, and instruction, and understanding.

—Proverbs 23:23

The economy of our world today has such a mixture of influences that control the national markets. I am reluctant to venture too far out on the financial ocean since it will reveal how little I understand about the various aspects of the monetary structures that drive our local economies. I do know that there are free markets and restricted (government-controlled) markets.

Relative to our scripture today, truth is presented as an extremely valuable commodity. It is grouped right alongside of wisdom, instruction, and understanding on the same shelf. It seems to me, this is to accommodate ready acquisition to these "compatible" products—compatible in the sense that you could have the truth but lack wisdom and have no understanding of the truth and not be able to use these to instruct others or to receive instruction yourself.

Yesterday's devotion included a statement that "truth never changes." Suppose you wanted sugar. But when you purchased it and took it home and put some in your coffee or tea or cake, you discovered it looked like sugar, was packaged like sugar, the cost was the same as (or more than) other sugar, but it tasted like *lemons* or *dill pickles*!

Truth never changes! But it is often imitated. I was in the tourist market area of a foreign country once when a young man showed me his arm festooned with about ten or twelve wristwatches, bright and shiny. "Hey, Mister! You like a buy nice watch? Really cheap. They are genuine imitation *Rolex*."

Genuine imitation—hmm. I believe that's what you call an oxymoron, and he must have thought I was the moron that he could trick into buying his product.

Before I go, consider this fact: Jesus said, "I am the way, the truth, and the life." The world is full of imitations, even imitations of Jesus. Just remember this: Jesus only was born of a virgin. Jesus only died and rose again, leaving the tomb empty. Jesus only was seen alive after his death by over five hundred people. Jesus only ascended into heaven with the promise to come back.

Jesus only cannot lie!

May your day be filled with the glory of His promise. I look forward to being with you again—down here or up there.

A Still, Small Voice

It's raining. As I usually do, I have been outside on my patio for a few minutes, allowing the freshness of a new day to wrap its arms around me. Most mornings, the crows are noisy—very noisy. Today, because of the rain (?), there are none. The silence is wonderful.

But as I sat, shivering in the early morning cold (I really was thinking of a good cup of coffee), I could hear the sweet melody of small birds. I realized then that probably the usual loud and raucous confusion of the crows caused these small creatures to remain silent.

Then I heard something else—no, not audibly with my ears but inwardly with my spirit. It seemed to be coming from somewhere outside of me, yet it was speaking deeply inside of me. You have, no doubt, already come to the obvious conclusion that the Spirit was speaking to me.

The subject matter was simple, easy to be understood: "How often do you allow the loud crying and cawing of dominant everyday issues to silence the voice of God that wants to speak into your life?" Immediately there was a quick inward urgency to "listen."

Elijah's great and strong breaking-rocks-in-pieces wind—no, not the earthquake nor the fire on the mountain—none of these element-based events revealed what God wanted to say to Elijah. But the LORD's will was there revealed in a still small voice.

For me this morning, I heard the lesson...and I learned.

The Biggest Word in
Any Language

I call heaven and earth to witness against you this
day, that ye shall soon utterly perish from off the
land whereunto ye go over Jordan to possess it;
But <u>if</u> from thence thou shalt seek the LORD thy
God, thou shalt find him, *if* thou seek him with
all thy heart and with all thy soul. When thou art
in tribulation, and all these things are come upon
thee, even in the latter days, *if* thou turn to the
LORD thy God, and shalt be obedient unto his
voice (for the LORD thy God is a merciful God);
he will not forsake thee, neither destroy thee, nor
forget the covenant of thy fathers which he sware
unto them.

—Deuteronomy 4:26, 29–31

As a very young preacher, an old Presbyter taught me that "a
text out of context is pretext." So let me put all this into context
here. First of all, Moses was getting ready to die. He'd been leading
these people for over forty years. In his mind, no doubt, he could
still feel the heaviness of carrying two tablets of stone down from the
mountain—tablets which contained a law written in the stone by the
finger of God!

It would appear that God had already judged Israel for sins
worthy of "utterly perish(ing) from off the land." But this was not
the case. Read verses 23–25, and you will see that God was giving

a warning with a full description of consequences for violating the commandments etched on the tablets of stone! "Take heed unto yourselves, lest ye forget the covenant of the LORD your God."

God is a merciful God, "not willing that any should perish but that all should come to repentance." Notice the promises of God in verses 29–30 of our text: If…if…and if. Now notice this: "For all the promises of God in him are yea, and in him Amen, unto the glory of God by us" (2 Corinthians 1:20).

One last verse for you today: "If my people, which are called by my name, shall humble themselves, and pray, and seek my face, and turn from their wicked ways; then will I hear from heaven, and will forgive their sin, and will heal their land" (2 Chronicles 7:14).

If my people will, then I will.

Two Simple Words

And Jesus, walking by the sea of Galilee, saw two brethren, Simon called Peter, and Andrew his brother, casting a net into the sea: for they were fishers. And he saith unto them, *Follow me*, and I will make you fishers of men. And they straightway left their nets, and followed him.

—Matthew 4:18–20

Now when Jesus saw great multitudes about him, he gave commandment to depart unto the other side. And a certain scribe came, and said unto him, Master, I will follow thee whithersoever thou goest. And Jesus saith unto him, The foxes have holes, and the birds of the air have nests; but the Son of man hath not where to lay his head. And another of his disciples said unto him, Lord, suffer me first to go and bury my father. But Jesus said unto him, *Follow me*; and let the dead bury their dead.

—Matthew 8:18–22

And as Jesus passed forth from thence, he saw a man, named Matthew, sitting at the receipt of custom: and he saith unto him, *Follow me*. And he arose, and followed him. And it came to pass, as Jesus sat at meat in the house, behold, many publicans and sinners came and sat down with him and his disciples. And when the Pharisees saw it, they said unto his disciples, Why eateth your Master with publicans and sinners? But when Jesus heard that, he said unto them, They that be whole need not a physician, but they that are sick. But go ye and learn what that meaneth, I will have mercy, and not sacrifice: for I am not come to call the righteous, but sinners to repentance.

—Matthew 9:9–13

Then said Jesus unto his disciples, If any man will come after me, let him deny himself, and take up his cross, and *follow me*. For whosoever will save his life shall lose it: and whosoever will lose his life for my sake shall find it. For what is a man profited, if he shall gain the whole world, and lose his own soul? or what shall a man give in exchange for his soul?

—Matthew 16:24–26

And, behold, one came and said unto him, Good Master, what good thing shall I do, that I may have eternal life? And he said unto him, Why callest thou me good? there is none good but one, that is, God: but if thou wilt enter into life, keep the commandments. He saith unto him, Which? Jesus said, Thou shalt do no murder, Thou shalt not commit adultery, Thou shalt not steal, Thou shalt not bear false witness, Honour thy father and thy mother: and, Thou shalt love thy neighbour as thyself. The young man saith unto him, All these things have I kept from my youth up: what lack I yet? Jesus said unto him, If thou wilt be perfect, go and sell that thou hast, and give to the poor, and thou shalt have treasure in heaven: and come and *follow me.* But when the young man heard that saying, he went away sorrowful: for he had great possessions.

—Matthew 19:16–22

All these encounters with Jesus are taken from the writings of the man named in the third sequence of events in Matthew 9. With variations based on the individual circumstances described by Matthew, each person involved in the encounter was told to engage in this act as a calling or way of life to accept the same code of conduct that Jesus manifested as authority in their life, even so far as to obey his call as authentic from God. This involved a total change in pursuit of livelihood for Peter and Andrew (Matthew 4:18–20).

It meant a serious study of the consequences of following Jesus, such as having no assurance of the provisions of life that even the creatures of the earth have (Matthew 8:18–22). Even Matthew's personal association with the Master, after he had left the tax collector's table, was called into question even though his new association was compared to a physician ministering to the sick (Matthew 9:9–13).

Even the intellectuals observed what really amounted to a very probing debate with a young man regarding personal religious upbringing. He was obviously very devout. But Jesus said, "You still haven't quite got it. You are lacking something. If thou wilt be perfect, go and sell that thou hast and give to the poor and come and *follow me.*" The crowd was in awe when the young man turned and went away sorrowful, for he had great possessions (Matthew 19:16–22).

No, one encounter was not omitted; it was not skipped. Rather, it was reserved for this purpose: to describe the struggle that you and I have with those two simple words—follow me. Before we can follow, there is the issue of self-denial. And then there is the life-changing, course-altering, all-encompassing matter that is ready for a decision—the cross. The cross. For all who would follow Jesus, there will always be the monumentally awesome knowledge that "if I follow Jesus, I must embrace the cross" (Matthew 16:24–26)!

Who, What, How!

> For God never said to any angel, "You are my
> Son, and today I have given you the honor that
> goes with that name." But God said it about
> Jesus. Another time he said, "I am his Father and
> he is my Son." And still another time—when his
> firstborn Son came to earth—God said, "Let all
> the angels of God worship him.
>
> —Hebrews 1:5–6 TLB

In the first chapter of Hebrews, a marvelous declaration about the supremacy of God's Son is made. In Hebrews 1:8, God (Spirit) gives expression to the amazing relationship he has with the Son (born of the Virgin Mary—true flesh of flesh). "That which is born of the flesh is flesh; and that which is born of the Spirit is spirit" (John 3:6). From his mother, he received fleshly attributes; however, his Father was Spirit, i.e., the supreme Deity or the very God! *This is the "Who."*

There is no attempt here to revisit any past Christmas sermon. I do want to establish in your understanding that the incarnation (the union of divinity with humanity in Jesus Christ) was part of God's plan from eternity past. His birth was nothing short of miraculous. From the Greek word *dunamis*, we have the thought of miraculous power (by implication a miracle itself); and the accompanying word *dunamai*, meaning "to be able" or "possible." So from the language itself, we get the conceptual definition that "God will come to earth in the form and substance of human flesh, and it shall be by the miraculous power of God." *This is the "What."*

Further to this, Mary received a divine assurance from the announcing angel who declared, "The Holy Ghost shall come upon thee, and the power of the Highest shall overshadow thee: therefore also that holy thing which shall be born of thee shall be called the Son of God. Then said Mary unto the angel, How shall this be, seeing I know not a man? And the angel answered and said unto her, 'With God nothing shall be impossible'" (Luke 1:34–37). This was not a transfer of power, rather an acknowledgment of the eternally existent plan for the revealing of that power among us! "And the Word was made flesh, and dwelt among us" (John 1:14). *This is the "How."*

> So we must listen very carefully to the truths we have heard, or we may drift away from them. For since the messages from angels have always proved true and people have always been punished for disobeying them, what makes us think that we can escape if we are indifferent to this great salvation announced by the Lord Jesus himself and passed on to us by those who heard him speak? (Hebrews 2:1–3 TLB)

> Everything of God gets expressed in Him, so you can see and hear him clearly. You don't need a telescope, a microscope, or a horoscope to realize the fullness of Christ, and the emptiness of the universe without him. When you come to him, that fullness comes together for you, too. His power extends over everything. (Colossians 2:9–10)

Walking through the Village of MUCHMORE

I have always wanted to go walking through the quaint little village of MUCHMORE. It probably isn't to be found in the province of Reality, but for sure, it is in the state of Truth. I've often seen it listed as a wonderful place to visit when I've been reading "The Master's Guide to Blessings." So if you'd like to go with me for a bit, I'm sure you will be happily surprised by the abundance of glory, power, and enlightenment.

Off we go now; no tickets needed. They were already paid, you know, by the Supreme Benefactor. As a matter of fact, you will receive *much more* than you even dreamed of. This first sight to behold is called The Overflow of Unity. The history of this event comes to us from a place and time long ago. You can read about it in "The Master's Guide to Blessings." It's found in the section known as Exodus in chapter 36:1–7. Going directly to the heart of this event, it seems a group of people (called Israelites) were asked to make donations to a renovation project at the local temple sanctuary. Now here is where we get to see the wonder of the people of MUCHMORE. The leaders of the project came to the General Project Overseer, a guy named Moses, and they said, "The people bring *much more* than enough." So Moses had to give the order to stop because they had enough. Amazing.

Can you imagine that?

The next item of discovery on our walk through MUCHMORE Village is called God's Marvellous Care For You. It is one of the largest display areas, so we will view it in two different sections. The first is called The Inner Man. It is interesting that the individual who presents this segment was an MD. That's right, a physician doctor. Luke goes right upfront with a challenge for your thinking. Listen: "Consider the ravens: for they neither sow nor reap, which neither have storehouse nor barn; and God feedeth them: how *much more* are ye better than the fowls?" He challenges your sense of self-worth. You are worth more than a bird, he says! What do you think?

Dr. Luke is quite skilled at his profession as you will notice. He now moves his focus, and yours, to the second section of this large display. It is called The Outward Man. It has to do with the necessities of life. Once again, his challenge is in your face, so to speak. "Consider the lilies how they grow: they toil not, they spin not; and yet I say unto you, that Solomon in all his glory was not arrayed like one of these. If then God so clothe the grass, which is to day in the field, and tomorrow is cast into the oven; how *much more* will he clothe you, O ye of little faith?" Isn't that great! He reminds you of God's marvelous care for you. You know He does, don't you?

Perhaps the strangest section in the village is called The Trial of Your Faith. It seems to be filled with contradicting issues—not bad, just hard to equate. Having custody of this section is a retired fisherman named Peter. Probably well-placed in his responsibility because he can be quick-tempered and opinionated—a real shoot-from-the-hip type of guy. Rumor has it that he once cut a guy's ear off with a sword while defending the Supreme Benefactor spoken of earlier. Listen to his tour guide spiel as he talks about trials and joy and the "appearing" of this One called Jesus Christ: "Wherein ye greatly rejoice, though now for a season, if need be, ye are in heaviness through manifold temptations: That the trial of your faith, being *much more* precious than of gold that perisheth, though it be tried with fire, might be found unto praise and honor and glory at the appearing of Jesus Christ:"

I say "always finish with style." This last section is one of a certain intellectual yet powerful presentation made by a fellow whose personal testimony involved bright lights, a heavenly voice, and get this, a name change from Saul of Tarsus to Paul. Eventually, the title of apostle was bestowed on him. Notice the very gracious finish he offers in summary of our tour through the village of MUCHMORE:

"For as by one man's disobedience many were made sinners, so by the obedience of one shall many be made righteous. Moreover, the law entered that the offence might abound. But where sin abounded, grace did *much more* abound. I sincerely hope you enjoyed the tour with me today. It was nice having you along."

Ernie Just Wanted to Go Home

And now, behold, I go bound in the spirit unto Jerusalem, not knowing the things that shall befall me there: Save that the Holy Ghost witnesseth in every city, saying that bonds and afflictions abide me. But none of these things move me, neither count I my life dear unto myself, so that I might finish my course with joy...

—Acts 20:22–24

Ernie just wanted to go home. Nobody knows why Ernie abandoned his family in the first place. Chris and Jennifer Trevino were cruising down a Texas highway at sixty miles per hour out in some of the most barren territory on earth when Ernie bailed out of the family truck without anybody knowing he was gone.

Did the black-and-white tomcat lean the wrong way on a corner somewhere out there in the desert six hundred miles west of his Victoria home? Possibly. Did he instinctively lunge at a passing insect without realizing that he would come down beyond the bed of the Trevino's moving truck? It's anybody's guess. By the time Ernie's owners missed him, they were many miles down the road. "We ought to go back and look for him," they said. But it was dark by then, and they didn't know where to start looking anyway.

Imagine their astonishment when, a week later, the errant Ernie showed up at their Texas home, all bloody, scratched, and footsore. Just how Ernie navigated that far through unfamiliar terrain, only God knew. Ernie's worn claws and the sores on his feet convinced his veterinarian that the plucky cat had covered lots of rough real estate.

Like everybody else who heard of Ernie's trek, the vet was amazed that a cat could cover so much distance in so short a time. "But," he said, "I wouldn't put anything past cats." With so many questions unanswered, one thing was clear: Ernie just wanted to go home. And so do we!

There's no telling what old Ernie went through as he tried to find his way home. I am sure that danger after danger dogged his steps. But when he finally arrived home, he found love, peace, safety, and a bowl of warm milk. You see, the things that had troubled Ernie along the way home couldn't follow him home.

As we make our way through this world, we are headed home. But along the way, there are many elements of this life that trouble us and hinder our progress. Evil bullies like death, disease, discouragement, depression, and the devil make our journey home treacherous and difficult. But with Paul, we can say, "I have fought a good fight, I have finished *my* course, I have kept the faith: Henceforth there is laid up for me a crown of righteousness, which the Lord, the righteous judge, shall give me at that day: and not to me only, but unto all them also that love his appearing."

Every one of the things that trouble us here will not be allowed to follow us home. Like Ernie, there will come a day when the journey will be over, and we will be safely at home in the Father's house. We will be in a place of peace, safety, and perfection. While I travel, I am troubled; but I know that those things that trouble you and me this morning, one day, will all come to an end. It will be better then. Battle scarred, travel worn, and weary we may be, but let's just keep traveling. Put a big sticker on your luggage for every trouble to see, one that says:

> You might trouble me here,
> but you can't follow me home!

A Close Call

The devotional text today is a story filled with high drama, sadness, romance, and bad and good decisions found in 1 Samuel 25:1–42. To be stated in a few brief paragraphs, this was what happened:

Saul was seeking David to kill him. He often was possessed with an evil spirit that motivated this wicked desire. David was hiding in the hills near the cave of Adullam. He had a group of six hundred men who were themselves desperados—debtors, men with legal issues, running from personal conflicts.

While hiding in the wilderness, David's men had occasioned to be in contact with shepherds of a very wealthy man named Nabal. His name meant fool. He had a beautiful wife who was very wise and a good judge of right and wrong (and their consequences). Her name was Abigail, meaning "source of joy."

David heard that Nabal was shearing his sheep. He knew that this meant there would be a lot of food prepared for the shearers. He sent ten young men to inquire of Nabal that he would consider sharing their feast since David's men had provided honest and true security for Nabal's flock in the wilderness.

Instead of a shared feast, David received insults and rejection from Nabal. David's young men delivered his message carefully to Nabal who tore into them. "Who is this David? Do you think I'm going to take good food prepared for my shearers and give it to men I've never laid eyes on?"

David's men got out of there quickly and told David what had happened. David was hot, boiling with anger. "Strap on your swords," he cried.

They all strapped on their swords and took off for Nabal's place—David and four hundred of his men.

Meanwhile, one of Nabal's young men told Abigail, Nabal's wife, what had happened. He vouched for David that they had protected them while they were in Carmel and Adullam. "Do something quickly. We are in big trouble."

Abigail flew into action. She took bread; wine; sheep, dressed ready for cooking; roasted grain; raisin cakes; fig cakes and had it loaded on some donkeys. "Go ahead of me. I'll be right behind you." As she was riding her donkey, descending into a ravine, David and his men were descending from the other end of the canyon. David was mumbling to himself, "That sure was a waste, guarding everything this man had out in the wilderness so that nothing he had was lost. And now he rewards me with insults!"

As soon as Abigail saw David, she leaped off her donkey and fell on her knees at his feet, saying, "My master, let me take the blame! Listen to what I have to say. I wasn't there when your young men arrived. Now take this gift that I, your servant girl, have brought you. Give it to the young men who follow you. Forgive my presumption! But GOD is at work in your life. GOD is going to set you up as the king over Israel."

And David said, "Blessed be GOD, the God of Israel. He sent you to meet me! And blessed be your good sense! Bless you for keeping me from taking matters into my own hands." This was a close call! Here are some quick observations:

- It's a sad thing when Nabal (fool) does not recognize what Abigail (source of joy) means to him.
- It may be that there are people in your life who are hiding in the hills for their own reasons, but God has put them there as his helpers for your sakes.
- They may not wear a robe and crown, and their Adullam may not contain a king's throne, but that does not mean they have not been anointed by God for his purpose one day.
- You may have many sheep to shear, but remember, it is not you that brings forth the lambs but the Creator God who

has ordered all things. It's not you that makes it happen; it's him! He is Lord overall.

- Anointed kings are still capable of making some very wrong decisions. Abigail had the good sense to prevent David from murdering Nabal simply because of personal insults. "Keep your head. Vengeance is mine," saith the Lord. God took Nabal's life ten days later. Soon thereafter, Abigail became David's advisor and wife.

Whoso findeth a wife findeth a good thing, and obtaineth favour of the LORD. (Proverbs 18:22)

Let's Go to Church!

I was glad when they said unto me, Let us go into the house of the LORD.

—Psalm 122:1

Let us go into the house of the Lord; the house of the sanctuary; the tabernacle, the place of divine worship; typical of the church of God. It is a house that He has built. it is He that makes it beautiful. He dwells there, meets His people there; He makes it a "city of refuge."

It is good for His people to stir up one another to go to His house. Some are slothful and backward. Some are lukewarm and indifferent. Some are worldly and carnally minded. Others think they already know it all and have no need to go there. But the truly gracious souls are glad when they are stirred up to go, both for their own account and for the account of others and because of the glory of God.

> And in thy fear will I worship. David's worship was never without fear—a reverent sense of God's greatness, power, and perfect holiness. (Psalm 5:7)

> I will worship toward thy holy temple, and praise thy name for thy lovingkindness and for thy truth: for thou hast magnified thy word above all thy name. (Psalm 138:2)

When the great Spanish Armada was ready to swoop down upon the English coast, Admiral Drake took some of his small ships and placed them where the wind would carry them right among the Spanish fleet. He filled the small vessels with combustible material and set them on fire. Then the wind took over (kind of like the Holy Ghost)! It just took the fire ships and drifted them up against the great Spanish galleons that floated high out of the water with their sides exposed to the air (and the flames), and one after another of the big monsters were soon ablaze, and a great victory was won without a blow being struck. So if we can get a red-hot Christian, full of music and praise unto Jehovah, and just let him go by the influence of the Holy Spirit right into the middle of the adversaries of truth, they won't know what to do. They don't know how to handle a man, woman, or a young person on fire!

Just Like a Donkey

And when they came nigh to Jerusalem, unto Bethphage and Bethany, at the mount of Olives, he sendeth forth two of his disciples, and saith unto them, Go your way into the village over against you: and as soon as ye be entered into it, ye shall find a colt tied, whereon never man sat; loose him, and bring him. And if any man say unto you, Why do ye this? say ye that the Lord hath need of him; and straightway he will send him hither. And they went their way, and found the colt tied by the door without in a place where two ways met; and they loose him.

And certain of them that stood there said unto them, What do ye, loosing the colt? And they said unto them even as Jesus had commanded: and they let them go. And they brought the colt to Jesus, and cast their garments on him; and he sat upon him. And many spread their garments in the way: and others cut down branches off the trees, and strawed them in the way. And they that went before, and they that followed, cried, saying, Hosanna; Blessed *is* he that cometh in the name of the Lord: Blessed be the kingdom of our father David, that cometh in the name of the Lord: Hosanna in the highest.

—Mark 11:1–10

This amazing passage records the triumphant entry of the Lord Jesus Christ into Jerusalem. The primary emphasis of this passage is the revelation of Jesus to Israel that He is their long awaited Messiah and their King.

I am interested in that little donkey. The Lord needed that donkey to fulfill His (the Lord's) mission here on earth. Isn't that amazing? Jesus is God, and He could have done this anyway He chose to. But He chose to use that small, little donkey. By the way, He is still using little creatures to get His work done on earth. He could assign the tasks to angels, but He chooses to work through people like you and me. Let me mention a few facts about that little donkey.

That donkey had to be redeemed. In our natural state, we were fit for nothing but the fires of hell. In our natural state, we were useless to God and separated from Him by a wide gulf of sin. That was our natural state. That may be how the Lord found us, but that is not the way He left us! When He saved us by His grace, He changed us completely!

He gave us His life. He bridged the gulf between us and Him. That is the only reason you and I have any usefulness to the Lord today because of the redeeming power of the blood of Jesus! Just so we understand, redemption is not an option, it is a necessity! Jesus put it this way to Nicodemus: "Ye must be born again." Without the new birth, you are lost in your sins.

That donkey had to be released. When Jesus told the disciples about the little donkey, He told them they would find it tied up. They were to untie the donkey and bring it to Jesus, which was what they did. That little donkey was bound, and it needed to be set free before the Lord could use it. When Jesus found us, we were just like that little donkey! Before you and I can be of any use to the Lord Jesus, the chains of our sins must be broken; and we must be set free.

That donkey had to be ruled. Someone had to take charge over that donkey. The donkey had never been broken to ride. It was a wild animal. That wild little donkey needed a master. It was wild, yet it submitted itself to the Lord Jesus and yielded to His control. That was a miracle. That is exactly what He expects of us! He is looking for total submission and total surrender from our lives.

Let's face the truth; some people have a real problem with authority. Who is your Master today? Is it you, or is it the Lord Jesus Christ? The Lord could save sinners and accomplish His work on earth just fine without us. Yet He chooses to use frail, human instruments for His glory.

At the Door

Behold, I stand at the door, and knock: if any man hear my voice, and open the door, I will come in to him, and will sup with him, and he with me.

—Revelation 3:20

Who stands at our door? We are reminded of an ancient principle of hospitality, which has largely fallen by the wayside of practicality in today's vulnerable society: "Be not forgetful to entertain strangers: for thereby some have entertained angels unawares" (Hebrews 13:2). By keeping an open heart and open house for strangers, some were privileged to entertain angels unexpectedly. Within the frame of our subject today, we may receive a visit from the Lord of angels if only we will let Him in.

No social distancing here. He is near enough to touch your door. Of course, we are speaking of the door to your heart, aren't we? We are not moved by anything that is far distant. Whether the visitor be coming for judgment or mercy, we take the matter lightly as long as he is far away. A distant enemy does not make us tremble. A distant friend fails to make us glad. When the one assigned as your security guard is distant, you tremble at danger; when he is near, you breathe freely again. How near the Son of God has come to us! He is more than a casual visitor. He is our Friend. He touches us, and we touch Him. We are close.

Ah, the door! Our own barrier—how far away the interrupter is kept. How near is our Friend "at the door." Look at the play of emotions. He, in great kindness, comes to the door. We, in great resistance, keep Him at the door. Rumor has it that some have given Him a nickname—the disturbing Christ. We have plans. His visit is not convenient right now. What will your neighbors, friends, family, business associates think if they see Him here?

He knocks for entrance. Besides coming near, He calls aloud. He does not permit you to forget His presence. Many things hinder the hearing. Hear and open. Hearing alone is not enough. The guilty refuse to open for Christ even when they hear Him knocking. They have hard thoughts of Him. They think He comes to demand a righteousness, which they cannot give, and to bind them over to the collection agency because they cannot pay. They forget that God is love, and Christ has come to give life. He comes to redeem you and save you.

Just as when you have called 911 in an emergency, you don't know the EMT technicians, the paramedics. But you know, they come as your help in time of need. Well let me introduce you to the one who stands at your door. His name is Jesus. He is here as your friend. Go ahead; open the door! It's okay.

> Open your heart and let Him in,
> God will remove all your sorrow and sin.
> He may not pass your way again,
> So open your heart and let Him come in.
> Take His hand, Take His nail-scarred hand,
> He will show you the Way.
> Jesus will be your dearest Friend,
> So, open your heart and let Him come in. (Marie Armenia)

Lost in Translation

And Enoch lived sixty and five years, and begat Methuselah: And Enoch walked with God after he begat Methuselah three hundred years, and begat sons and daughters: And all the days of Enoch were three hundred sixty and five years: And Enoch walked with God: and he was not; for God took him.

—Genesis 5:21–24

By faith Enoch was translated that he should not see death; and was not found, because God had translated him: for before his translation he had this testimony, that he pleased God.

—Hebrews 11:5

Language is a funny thing. Most of the time, we understand what we hear in our own language, but when languages are translated, sometimes the results are very humorous, even hilariously funny. Consider the following examples:

- In an advertisement by a Hong Kong dentist: Teeth extracted by the latest Methodists.
- In a Copenhagen airline ticket office: We take your bags and send them in all directions.
- An English sign in Tokyo, translated from Japanese, warning motorists to watch for pedestrians says, "When a pas-

senger of the foot heave in sight, tootle the horn. Trumpet at him melodiously at first, but if he still obstacles your passage, then tootle him with vigor."

Sometimes the true meaning of what is being said is lost in translation. Our text speaks of "translation" three times. It refers to the translation of a man name Enoch. When Enoch was translated, he was also lost in translation. He was lost to the world, but he was found in another.

The word *translated* means "to transfer, to transport, to change sides, to carry over, to remove." The word *translation* refers to a transport. It carries the idea of "moving something from one place to another." So when the Bible says that Enoch was translated, it means that he was transported from one place to another. He changed sides. He was carried over. He was removed from this world and transferred to a new world.

Enoch's experience speaks to us. The day will come when we will also be translated. We must be ready to leave this world. Enoch didn't know when he would leave, but he was ready when his time came to go. We need to be ready as well. Life is fleeting. James 4:14 reminds us that it is like the morning fog. It is up to us to make every moment count for God and to be ready when He comes.

We have such a blessed future! The world is falling apart around us. Our governments have lost their bearings. Our economy is in the tank. Our morals are bankrupt. Many churches have abandoned truth. Our families are in trouble. Things look bad. But the redeemed saints of God still have their blessed hope. Our God is still on the throne, and our Lord is still coming for His people. So keep walking with God. One day, as you're walking with Him and you're tired and weary, He'll say, "You know, we've walked so far. We're closer to my home than yours. Why don't you come on home with me!" And you will be gone!

The Great Escape

The words of the Preacher, the son of David, king in Jerusalem.

Vanity of vanities, saith the Preacher, vanity of vanities; all is vanity. I the Preacher was king over Israel in Jerusalem. And I gave my heart to seek and search out by wisdom concerning all things that are done under heaven: this sore travail hath God given to the sons of man to be exercised therewith. I have seen all the works that are done under the sun; and, behold, all is vanity and vexation of spirit.

—Ecclesiastes 1:1–2, 12–14

What does this mean? Vanity is defined as something that has no substance, emptiness, meaninglessness, worthlessness, and futility. All is vanity because everything in life is temporary.

Think about the vanity of money and possessions. Solomon wrote that one who loves money will not be satisfied with it, nor is there satisfaction for one who loves abundance with its income. In fact, it becomes a source of severe affliction and stress.

Life is not defined by things. In Mark 10, the rich young person who did everything to keep Christ's commandments and desired to know how to gain eternal life was told he lacked one thing; he needed to sell whatever he had and take up his cross and follow Christ. Instead, he went away grieved, for he had great possessions.

We are all born with an ego. The ego (pride) is the false sense of who we think we are. Pride is a master at causing us to think better of ourselves than we should. It persuades us to resist the path of righteousness and prevents us from doing right. We are convinced with good intentions to become better people, better helpers, better servants of Jesus Christ, and teachers of God's word.

- But with no conscious invitation, our ego entices us or encourages us to stray.
- It keeps us slightly askew from the straight road that we intended to walk.
- The ego loves to keep us in a vicious cycle of negativity.
- We become discouraged, scornful of our own actions, and contemptible to ourselves.

All of these attitudes are arrived at because of stinkin' thinkin'. We suffer due to our ego. We must learn to *let go* of our *ego*! We must learn to live beyond the ego in total surrender to Jesus Christ. Paul said in Galatians 2:20, "I am crucified with Christ: nevertheless I live; yet not I, but Christ liveth in me." We must become one with Jesus Christ. Take on baptism in Jesus Name; take on His suffering, his death; be filled with the Holy Spirit!

The solution comes from within. To surrender ourselves to Jesus Christ, we must let go of self-defeating thought patterns and acknowledge and control our ego. This surrender is a personal pivot point that enables the control of our lives to be worked out by Almighty God. He is infinitely greater than we ourselves. Yield to him. Abandon your way for His way, and escape the insanity of vanity of this world.

Make the decision to follow Christ. After all, He is the Way, the Truth, and the Life! Keep walking toward the city!

Consider the Goose

Go to the ant, thou sluggard; consider her ways, and be wise.

—Proverbs 6:6

Consider the lilies of the field, how they grow.

—Matthew 6:28

God speaks to us in so many ways. To Elijah, God spoke in a still, small voice. To John on Patmos, God spoke with "a great voice, as of a trumpet." Jesus chose to speak in parables, refusing to speak to the people except by this means. So if we are reminded of the ant and if he urged us to consider the lilies, then to stimulate your thinking today, I would ask you to consider the goose.

Geese are among the larger birds living today. Many averages twelve to eighteen pounds. As they gather to feed prior to winter, they tend to overeat, making them fat quickly; thus, they become easy prey for their enemies. Each year, they shed all their old feathers and grow a new set. Over the years, I've seen a lot of people trying to change their feathers without the benefit of personal growth.

We have all heard the loud cries of a flock of geese overhead. They fly in a wedge or V formation. As a rule, they never fly alone. I like to think the V formation stands for victory! Ecclesiastes 4:9–10 says, "Two are better than one; because they have a good reward for their labour. For if they fall, the one will lift up his fellow: but woe to him that is alone when he falleth; for he hath not another to help him up." Verse 12 continues, "And if one prevail against him, two shall withstand him; and a threefold cord is not quickly broken."

If one begins to fall, the geese close by will circle around and fly along with it, encouraging and supporting. If it should fall, one or two will descend with it to the ground to care for and guard and protect it until recovery is made. Should it die, they will mourn for a period of time before rising again to join a flock onward in its migration.

Geese have intimidating natural enemies. They are the natural prey of foxes, wolves, and coyotes. The time the enemy strikes most often is when the goose is on the ground. Therefore, it is so important that a vigilant watch be kept, lest while the flock is feeding, predators break in upon them and destroy many. The apostle Peter put this into a very sobering application for you and me in the church.

> Be sober, be vigilant; because your adversary the devil, as a roaring lion walketh about, seeking whom he may devour. (1 Peter 5:8)

As they fly in formation, they shift forward (not backward) and give the leader a rest from the toil of first position. This is called renewal. In the Church, it's called *revival*. Do you ever move forward to shift some of the load of the Pastor to yourself? Do you ever volunteer your assistance? Do you ever just come alongside with an offer to support and help during an especially difficult time?

This is the work of the Paraclete, the Comforter, the one who comes alongside. You know, you could be a great Holy Ghost friend to someone by just coming alongside for a moment and shifting their load. How do you spell relief?—by becoming a friend of consolation. If you need some instruction in this, ask Barnabas.

The next time you hear *honk*! *honk*! don't look around. Look up! You might see a V for *victory*!

This Is My King

The Bible says my king is a seven-way king. He is the king of the Jews; that's a racial king. He is the king of Israel, and that's a national king. He is the king of righteousness. He is the king of the ages. He is the king of heaven. He is the king of glory. He is the King of kings. And He is the Lord of lords. That's my king. Do you know him?

David said the heavens declare the glory of God, and the firmament shows his handiwork. My king is a sovereign king. No means of measure can define his limitlessness. No farseeing telescope can bring into visibility the coastline of his shoreless supply. No barrier can hinder him from pouring out his blessings. He is enduring and strong, and He is entirely sincere. He is eternally steadfast. He is immortally graceful. He is entirely powerful. He is impartially merciful. Do you know him?

He is the greatest phenomenon that has ever crossed the horizon of this world. He is God's son, and He is the sinner's Savior. He is the Son of peace of civilization. He stands in the solitude of himself. He's awesome, and He's unique. He's unparalleled, and he's unprecedented.

He is the loftiest idea in literature. He is the highest personality in philosophy. He is the supreme problem in high criticism. He is the fundamental doctrine of true theology. He is the absolute necessity of spiritual religion. He is the miracle of the age. He is the superlative of everything good that you choose to call him. He is the only one qualified to be an all-sufficient Savior. I wonder if you know him today.

He supplies strength for the weak. He is available for the tempted and tried. He sympathizes, and He heals. He strengthens, and He saves. He is God. He died on the cross, but He rose from the dead. He loves the lost. He cleansed the leper. He forgives sinners. He discharges debtors. He delivers the captives. He defends the feeble. He blesses the young. He serves the unfortunate. He regards the aged. He rewards the diligent. He beautifies the meek, and I just wonder, do you know Him?

This is my king, and he is the key to knowledge. He is the wellspring of wisdom. He is the doorway of deliverance. He is the pathway of peace. He is the roadway of righteousness. He is the highway of holiness. He is the gateway to glory. Do you know him?

His office is manifold, and His promise is sure. His life is matchless. His goodness is limitless. His mercy is everlasting. His love never changes. His word is enough. His grace is sufficient. His reign is righteous. His yoke is easy, and His burden is light. I wish I could describe Him to you, but He is indescribable. He is incomprehensible. He is invincible, and He is irresistible. Have you met Him?

Well you can't get him out of your mind. You can't get him off your hands. You can't outlive him, and you can't live without Him. The Pharisees couldn't stand Him, but they found out they couldn't stop him. Pilate couldn't find any fault in Him. The witnesses couldn't get their testimonies to agree. Herod couldn't kill him. Death couldn't handle Him. And the grave couldn't hold Him. That's my king.

And "thine is the kingdom and the power and the glory forever and forever and forever, world without end." If you don't know Him, you are cordially invited to a "Meet and Greet" this Sunday at church!

Bruised Reeds, Smoking Flax, and Broken Hearts

Behold my servant, whom I have chosen; my beloved, in whom my soul is well pleased: A bruised reed shall he not break, and smoking flax shall he not quench, till he send forth judgment unto victory.

—Matthew 12:18, 20

The Spirit of the Lord GOD *is* upon me; because the LORD hath sent me to bind up the brokenhearted...

—Isaiah 61:1

Bruised reeds. What is the picture? What is the lesson? What is the meaning? I would suggest this is a description of the nature of Jesus's Spirit and ministry. He was not sent for the destruction of the bruised, the hurt, or the injured. It was not His nature to cut off that which could be more easily destroyed than restored. Imagine, if you will, walking along a pathway through a patch of reeds along the wayside; by some means, one was bruised and bent across the pathway. The easiest thing to do would be to grasp it in one's hands and complete the process of demolition. Pull it apart at the bruise, and toss the separated portion to one side, taking no thought of the injury done.

The picture of Jesus's ministry was not like this. He would not do this. Instead, He would tenderly place the injured section back in place. He would perhaps bind it with a splint to hold it in the right position so that the healing process could take place. I have used a bit of scotch tape to bind a broken flower to its stem so that it could continue the process of spreading beauty. The reed, possibly accounted as unworthy by most, would thus be restored. In my backyard was a lovely pear tree—lovely but broken and splitting right in the center of the primary limbs. With a bit of gray duct tape, the break was mended, and the tree continued to display its beauty and to bear fruit!

Smoking flax. Probably, most will have little firsthand knowledge of this. The days of kerosene and coal oil lamps are nearly gone. Nevertheless, the wick of the oil lantern will begin to smoke as the lamp begins to run out of fuel. The wick, in Bible days, was made of flax and was placed in the bowl containing the oil with only the tip sticking out the top of the lamp. The intent was for the wick to soak up the oil, bring it to the top and for the oil to burn not the wick. The wick would last a long time, so long as there was plenty of oil in the lamp. However, when the oil ran out and was not replenished, then the wick would begin to smolder because it would be burning instead of the oil. In many places around the world, methods more primitive than this are still the instrument of light.

This picture illustrates the ministry of Jesus. Two things can be done with a smoking flax wick: It can easily be snuffed out. Moisten two fingers, and simply pinch it out. On the other hand, one can carefully gain access to the reservoir, carefully pour in some more oil; put everything back in proper position; and as soon as the oil is absorbed by the smoking wick, it will burst into flame and give forth the light for which it is intended. This is the imagery of scripture: "Be watchful, and strengthen the things which remain, that are ready to die" (Revelation 3:2).

Broken hearts. The picture of His ministry is to "heal or bind up" broken hearts. The image is one of restoration of that which is "broken." It is one of healing hurts. It is one of ministering to those in need. Hearts can be broken by one's failures and the abuse of others. In either case, the hurt and damage is real and needs some binding up. Such was and is the nature of Jesus's ministry.

Life Is Short

Job asked, "Are not my days few" (Job 10:20)? He answered his own question, "Man that is born of a woman is of few days, and full of trouble" (Job 14:1).

Life is described in several ways throughout Scripture:

- water spilled on the ground (2 Samuel 14:14);
- a pilgrimage (Genesis 47:9);
- but a step between life and death (1 Samuel 20:3);
- a shadow (1 Chronicles 29:15);
- swifter than a weaver's shuttle (Job 7:6);
- like the wind (Job 7:7);
- like grass that grows in the morning, and in the evening it is cut down; and withers (Psalm 90:6);
- a morning fog—here a little while, and then gone (James 4:14).

LORD, remind me how brief my time on earth will be. Remind me that my days are numbered, and that my life is fleeing away. My life is no longer than the width of my hand. An entire lifetime is just a moment to you; human existence is but a breath. We are merely moving shadows, and all our busy rushing ends in nothing. We heap up wealth for someone else to spend. (Psalm 39:4–6 NLT)

I suppose, this entire devotion should be taken with a grain of salt, considering that the writer was once young and is now old. (I can't even use the cliché, "But I don't feel old.") Some time ago, I was speaking with one of my young "preacher boys." He was talking about his plans for growth—excellent plans by the way; but they were going to consume most of his allotted twenty-four hours in a day. I commented that, yes, it's far more noble to "burn out" for the Lord than "rust out" for nothing. But there is the fact that each of us have only one candle (life) to burn; and if the candle is lighted at both ends, you will get twice as much light but only for half as long.

This homely little homily acquires much more traction if there are children and family involved. I do not hesitate to direct our attention to the devotional title: "Life Is Short." Man does an awful lot of things (some of which are exactly that—*awful!*) just to stretch the time span called life.

Did you know that Moses wrote more words in the Bible than any other person? Most of those words are in the books of Genesis, Exodus, Leviticus, Numbers, and Deuteronomy. And (back to my devotional path) Moses also wrote a Psalm: Psalm 90. In his one and only Psalm, he focused on the length of life. First, he established the length of God's existence. Look, "even from everlasting to everlasting, thou art God." Then he gets down to the business of life (and death).

> For a thousand years in thy sight are but as yester-day when it is past. (Psalm 90:4)

> The days of our years are threescore years and ten (seventy); and if by reason of strength they be fourscore (eighty) years yet is their strength labour and sorrow; for it is soon cut off, and we fly away. (Psalm 90:10)

> So teach us to number our days, that we may apply our hearts unto wisdom. (Psalm 90:12)

> Life is lived by the seconds, minutes, hours, days, weeks, months, and years. They are more precious than rubies and diamonds. Spend your time wisely.

The Gallery of the Ages

There is therefore now no condemnation to them which are in Christ Jesus, who walk not after the flesh, but after the Spirit. For the law of the Spirit of life in Christ Jesus hath made me free from the law of sin and death.

—Romans 8:1–2

I will give you three rapid-fire positive statements which will knock your socks off right at the opening of this little stroll in the Word of God.

- Our disabilities and handicaps need not limit our usefulness.
- No failure need be permanent.
- The future can be better than the past.

Let's go to an Art Gallery! The Apostle Paul picks up palette and brush and, using the oil paint of the Holy Spirit, begins painting a series of portraits for each saint of God to benefit thereby. First in the series is his masterpiece (found in Romans 5:19), which I will call *The Works of Two Men;* for in it he depicts how many were made sinners by one man's (Adam's) disobedience while simultaneously revealing how, by another man's (Christ's) obedience, many shall be made righteous.

Hanging next to that painting will be the second in this four-part series, which is found in Romans 6:5–6, I call *Victory over Tyranny.* This painting is rather dark. Standing prominently in the background is an old, rugged looking cross. Blood stains and the

108

elements of pain and suffering are evident in every corner and surface of the painting. But occupying the central space in the bottom foreground of the artwork lies a hideous-looking caricature crumpled in defeat with another figure resplendent in victory who, though bearing the marks of a hard-fought bloody battle, is surrounded by a multitude of joyously rejoicing people. Many of them have the evidence of slavery—chains, marks of bondage, weariness—but no longer enslaved. They are gloriously happy.

Though hanging separately, portrait # 3 seems almost to be attached or at least an extension of the previous portrait. This portrait is described by Paul in Romans 7:24 to which I will ascribe the title of *Between Two Worlds*. The oil paint of the Holy Spirit depicts three scenes. On the one hand, it is a horde of demonic creatures grasping, tugging, pulling, swearing, drinking, and doing drugs with immorality rampant everywhere. On the other hand, it is a band of angels, holy in appearance, armed with swords (which look like, yes, Bibles.) These angelic beings seem to glow with a light from within. A heavenly music emanates from their grouping. But the central figure, pulled from both sides, has such a tormented, tortured look of agony and inner turmoil. One can only imagine the actual battle that transpired within the heart of that one figure, who strangely enough, looked strikingly like me.

As we complete our tour through the *Gallery of the Ages*, we pause before the final portrait in this series so masterfully portrayed by the apostle. There is only one type of person featured in this portrait. Romans 8 is a portrait of an optimistic heir, claiming what is rightfully his. Things are so different now. In chapter 7, the personal pronoun "I" is used thirty-three times, and the Holy Ghost is not mentioned once. But those featured in this painting, which shall be called *A New Creature,* appear to be free of bondage, no more encumbrances. The *Holy Spirit* is mentioned eighteen times, and *I* is mentioned only two times. The words no *condemnation* do not mean a lack of criminal judgment but rather civil judgment. There are no lienholders to post a claim against them who are in Christ. No dead hand from the past is going to come out of the coffin of condemnation to stir up the tranquility of the present. Recently, from the battlefields of life, they are filled with a joy that is so obviously unspeakable, and they are so full of glory. And why not! Clutched in the hand of those joyful souls is a paper bearing their name and stamped *Paid In Full* and signed in blood of Jesus!

Angels Even in Sodom

And there came two angels to Sodom at even.

—Genesis 19:1

I will therefore put you in remembrance, though ye once knew this, how that the Lord, having saved the people out of the land of Egypt, afterward destroyed them that believed not. And the angels which kept not their first estate, but left their own habitation, he hath reserved in everlasting chains under darkness unto the judgment of the great day. Even as Sodom and Gomorrah, and the cities about them in like manner, giving themselves over to fornication, and going after strange flesh, are set forth for an example, suffering the vengeance of eternal fire.

—Jude 1:5–7

Angels in Sodom! What a contrast. The brightest and holiest of the Lord's servants ministering in the darkest and wickedest of cities. Even slum work may become angelic. These messengers of mercy and of judgment are examples to all who desire to be involved in rescuing the perishing.

Notice where they went. They went to Sodom, a city reeking with iniquity; and they went conscious that their eyes and ears must see and hear things that would pierce their souls with an agony of pain and distress. But they were prepared to suffer; they were willing even to abide in the street all night. Those who would seek the salvation of others must be ready to sacrifice their own comfort and ease.

We should also note why they went. They went because the Lord sent them. They did not go because they felt that the wickedness of the city demanded that something should be done or because they had nothing else more urgent to do. No. They went with a definite commission at the bidding of the Lord. They realized that the work was not theirs but God's. They had come in His Name and in His strength to do His will among them, and it would be done. The servants of Christ would soon grow weary in well-doing if they did not have this perfect assurance that they were in the very place and doing the very work He had sent them to do. The next matter for consideration must not stand on any other foundation than this.

This was what they went to do. They went to preach instant salvation and coming judgment. "Up, get yourself out of this place, for the Lord will destroy this city." They had no scheme of social reform to propose. Those Sodomites were condemned already, not by man, not by angels but by their own deeds! There was no alternative left for them but to escape or perish. The eyes of these heaven-sent messengers were wide awake to the real facts of the case so that they could do nothing else but press home their one message of warning and hope. They spoke and acted as those who believed in the wrath to come and who saw the peril of those who would linger through indecision. There was no time like "now| to them: "Behold, now is the day of salvation!" So urgent were these evangelists that they literally laid hold of Lot, his wife, and his two daughters.

Soul winning and personal evangelism must be wrapped in an aura of urgency if it is to be effective. These felt a pressing necessity if souls were to be rescued from the approaching doom. Why should preachers of the gospel not be as earnest and as urgent as these two angels were? Did they not have a definite a message to deliver? Is there not the same danger of destruction awaiting those who believe not, who obey not the gospel?

"Rescue the perishing, care for the dying, snatch them in pity from sin and the grave. Weep o'er the erring one, lift up the fallen. Tell them of Jesus, the mighty to save."

If this world is a Sodom, then you stand as one of its angels; and you have the only message of salvation!

Make No Mistake About It

And when they came to Nachon's threshing floor, Uzzah put forth his hand to the ark of God, and took hold of it; for the oxen shook it. And the anger of the LORD was kindled against Uzzah; and God smote him there for his error; and there he died by the ark of God.

—2 Samuel 6:6–7

The KJV Bible does not utilize the word *mistake*, rather it incorporates the word *error*. Uzzah died for his error. Students fail tests and even flunk classes because of errors made on their tests. Athletes commit errors (especially in baseball) and can cause the game to be lost. Erratophobia, or errophobia, is the fear of making mistakes. Everybody makes mistakes, but not everyone has the fear of making mistakes. Are you afraid to make a mistake? If you are, think about a lady named Bette Nesmith who cashed in on other people's mistakes. Bette had a good secretarial job at a bank in Dallas when she began thinking of ways she could more effectively correct typing errors. She knew that artists who worked with oil paintings just painted over their mistakes. She began experimenting. And having a bit of art experience, she concocted a white mixture to paint over her typing errors. Soon, all the secretaries in her building were using what she then called Mistake Out. She felt it was a proven product, so she attempted to sell the idea to marketing agencies and various companies (including IBM); but they all turned her down. She then decided to market her idea herself. Her kitchen became her factory. Bette Nesmith finally got the attention of Gillette; they bought her out for $47.5 million. That's right, those little 0.6 oz bottles of Liquid Paper turned out to be quite valuable. If a company was willing to pay nearly $50 million for a product that covers mistakes, know for certain that there are a lot of people besides you who make mistakes.

A young man from a wealthy family was about to graduate from high school. The custom of the wealthy parents was to give a brand-new car to their graduating student on graduation day. The boy fully expected this would be true for him as well. He had spent months talking about cars and looking at them with his father. Just a week before graduation, this father and son found what appeared to be the perfect car. The young man was certain he would see the car in his driveway. Yet when he opened his father's graduation present, it was a Bible. He was so mad that he threw down the Bible and stormed out of the house. He never reconciled with his father and remained estranged and offended until the day his father died. As the son went through his father's belongings, he came across the Bible his father had given him years ago. He brushed off the dust and opened it. To his surprise and horror, he found a cashier's check between the pages of Scripture. It was dated the day of his graduation for the exact amount of the car he and his dad had chosen together. God's greatest gifts are still found in the pages of Scripture, but we sometimes allow greed to destroy relationships and divert our attention elsewhere.

Augustine (AD 354–430) said, "God wants to give us something, but cannot, because our hands are full—there's nowhere for him to put it." When we feel as though God's blessings are missing from our lives, we need to examine our hands and see if they are open to receive or clutched around something that we refuse to let go. Bette Nesmith was made wealthy by creating a white liquid to cover mistakes on a paper. You and I are made wealthy because Jesus's red blood covers the black sins and makes them white as snow. Now, IBM, don't make the same mistake twice! Don't turn down this product...market it! It will change the world!

Young man, young woman, look inside that Bible. Pressed between the pages are true riches.

The Day I Got "Zanderized"

(That's What His Dad Says Happened to Me)

It happened at the School of Missions in Carlinville, Illinois, in August 2002. I was sitting at the dinner table designated for all the September people when the Regional Director for Europe/Middle East exploded confetti all over my head—you know, the little poppers that have a string that you pull. Then *pow*! the cap popped off, and shredded confetti flew everywhere. Well that was how I got "Zanderized."

You see, every year at the SOM, we had a big birthday bash. The wives of the RD's decorated the tables according to the theme of the month. The July table was decorated appropriately with an Independence Day motif; and it was also appropriately adjacent to the September table, which had a back-toschool theme. Hence, I became a convenient target for the guerrilla tactics of the abovementioned RD.

Of course, the loud bang and the flying confetti attracted a lot of attention. I soon noticed Alexander Starin (better known as Zander), the six-year-old son of Middle Eastern missionaries Mark and Mariann Starin sidling up to the July table. He slowly made his way around the table, looking at the flags and banners, the red, white, and blue hats, and the poppers laying loosely all over the table. Picking one up, I handed it to him and silently pointed at Robert

Rodenbush, motioning to Alexander that he should pull the string and pop it over Rodenbush's head (not very Biblical, but hey, this was guerrilla warfare!).

Alexander refused. He just stood there, shaking his head. After much whispering and urging him on to glory and valor, I asked young Alexander Starin, "Why not?" That's when he got me but good. With arms akimbo, he looked me square in the eye, took a deep breath, and said, "It's called conviction!" *Pow!*

Oh, the things God can accomplish when conviction enters. Men will walk away from a determined judgment when conviction finds none of them to be without sin. Conviction casts the qualifications for stone throwing against the backdrop of carnal motives, self-promotion, and self-righteousness. Without sin? Conviction uses a finely tipped brush when it paints upon the canvas of man's conscience. Conviction never addresses its letters "General Delivery."

Conviction is effective only when it is allowed access to the conscience. Paul warned us that in the latter times, some would depart from the faith, giving heed to seducing spirits and doctrines of devils; speaking lies in hypocrisy; having their conscience seared with a hot iron. The metaphor is from the practice of branding slaves or criminals; the branding of the criminals was on the brow. The allusion here is doubtless to the effect of applying a hot iron to the skin. The cauterized part becomes rigid and hard and is dead to sensitivity. So it is with the conscience.

We hear remarks about the "national conscience." The national conscience, however, does not exist where there is no individual conscience. David wisely said, "The wicked shall be turned into hell and all the nations that forget God." I had the honor of being asked by an MLA to pray at a local school recently to commemorate the events of September 11. In this politically correct (but spiritually incorrect) age, it was necessary to write out my prayer for submission and preapproval by the school board. It was rejected out of hand, and the entire commemorative ceremony was scrubbed. Why? The prayer sounded too religious, and the ceremony was too structured around God. Pardon me?

Where was political correctness on 9/11 when men and women alike wept and unashamedly knelt in the streets to pray for the mercy of God? Where was the reluctance to call on God then?

So quickly we forget our dependence on the Lord. So quickly we lose our aversion to the red-hot branding iron that sears the conscience.

Occasionally, there is erected a monument, which rises above the mendacity of sinful humanity. It outshines the short-lived luminaries of a people gone astray. Such is the monument erected by God Himself, a landmark of such majestic proportions yet plainly beautiful in its message. It can be read—indeed should be read—by all who envision a better tomorrow. The monument is framed in Holy writ, and it says, "If my people, which are called by my name, shall humble themselves, and pray, and seek my face, and turn from their wicked ways; then will I hear from heaven, and will forgive their sin, and will heal their land" (2 Chronicles 7:14).

Every "Though" Has Its' "Yet"

> Every block of stone has a statue inside it, and it is the task of the sculptor to discover it.
>
> —Michelangelo

Consider, if you will, the art craft of sculpting. The sculptor takes a hammer and chisel and applies them forcefully to the block of stone. He does this over and over and over relentlessly. Rather than thinking of the stone being turned into the statue he had in his mind, he imagined that there was a statue already trapped inside the stone, waiting for him to release it. His job was to chisel away anything that wasn't a part of the beautiful sculpture trapped inside. In a nutshell, instead of turning a rock into a statue, he was releasing a statue from the rock. The hammer and chisel are essential to the stone if a sculpture is to emerge.

Point and counterpoint. To and fro. All working toward the same goal—sculptor and hammer, hammer and chisel, chisel and stone. Heavy blow by heavy blow, slowly the image locked within the stone is released until, finally, it is presented as a living stone! Sir Isaac Newton's third law stated that "for every action, there is an equal and opposite reaction." For a moment, allow me to illustrate this by first giving two definitions: one for the word *though* and one for the word *yet*.

Though means potentially existing in the future or in existence now. *Yet* is defined as "in spite of what may or may not happen or may be happening now."

Here are some examples: To demonstrate his confidence in God, Job said, "Though he slay me, yet will I trust in him." And to demonstrate his confidence in God's power, Job said, "And though after my skin worms destroy this body, yet in my flesh shall I see God."

Peter said unto Jesus, "Though all men shall be offended because of thee, yet will I never be offended." Jesus said unto him, "Verily I say unto thee, That this night, before the cock crow, thou shalt deny me thrice." Peter said unto him, "Though I should die with thee, yet will I not deny thee."

Once again, Peter hammered chisel against stone to declare his confidence in the invisible God. "Blessed be the God and Father of our Lord Jesus Christ, which according to his abundant mercy hath begotten us again unto a lively hope by the resurrection of Jesus Christ from the dead that the trial of our faith might be found unto praise and honor and glory at the appearing of Jesus Christ: Whom having not seen, ye love; in whom, though now ye see him not, yet believing, ye rejoice with joy unspeakable and full of glory."

And then Paul chiseled away at the marvelous image of His renewing power "for which cause we faint not; but though our outward man perish, yet the inward man is renewed day by day."

But John the beloved brought all these examples to a full declaration of faith fulfilled in steadfastness. Listen to his witness: "Beloved, [though] now are we the sons of God, and it doth not yet appear what we shall be: but we know that, when he shall appear, we shall be like him; for we shall see him as he is."

One day, the last blow of hammer and chisel upon stone shall release the image of the one that the sculptor has been seeking to release. To borrow from John: "But we know that, when he shall appear, we shall be like him; for we shall see him as he is."

New Heavens and a New Earth

I am creating new heavens and a new earth; everything of the past will be forgotten. Celebrate and be glad forever! I am creating a Jerusalem, full of happy people. I will celebrate with Jerusalem and all of its people; there will be no more crying or sorrow in that city. No child will die in infancy; everyone will live to a ripe old age. Anyone a hundred years old will be considered young, and to die younger than that will be considered a curse.

—Isaiah 65:17–20 (CEV)

One hundred years!—what a difference a century can make! It doesn't sound very long, yet it boggles the mind when it is considered with all its changes. Here are some of the statistics taken from a hundred years ago:

The average life expectancy was forty-seven years. More than 95 percent of all births took place at home. Ninety percent of all doctors had no college education. Instead, they attended so-called medical schools, many of which were condemned in the press and by the government as "sub-standard."

Five leading causes of death were pneumonia and influenza, tuberculosis, diarrhea, heart disease, and stroke. Marijuana, heroin, and morphine were all available over the counter at the local corner drugstores. Back then, pharmacists said, "Heroin clears the complexion, gives buoyancy to the mind, regulates the stomach and bowels, and is, in fact, a perfect guardian of health." It was shocking to say the least!

Only 14 percent of the homes had a bathtub. Only 8 percent of the homes had a telephone. And no wonder, a three-minute call from Denver to New York City cost eleven dollars!

The tallest structure in the world was the Eiffel Tower! There were only 8,000 cars in the US and only 144 miles of paved roads. The maximum speed limit in most cities was 10 mph. The population of Las Vegas was 30.

The average wage in the US was 22¢ per hour, with the average worker making between $200 and $400 per year. A competent accountant earned $2,000 per year; a dentist, $2,500 per year; a veterinarian between $1,500 and $4,000 per year; and a mechanical engineer about $5,000 per year. Canada passed a law that prohibited poor people from entering their country for any reason. Two out of every ten adults couldn't read or write, and only 6 percent of all Americans had graduated from high school.

Sugar cost 4¢ a pound. Eggs were 14¢ a dozen. Coffee was 15¢ a pound. Most women only washed their hair once a month and used borax or egg yolks for shampoo. Crossword puzzles, canned beer, and iced tea hadn't been invented yet.

With all these fantastic changes, I see no mention of the greatest life-changing event, I believe, in the entire scope of the passage of these years from one century to the next. Of course, I'm referring to the outpouring of the Holy Ghost, first on New Year's evening 1899 at Stones Folly in Kansas. It was at a prayer meeting conducted in the Bible college of Reverend Charles Parham when some of the students began speaking in other tongues, marvelously filled with the Holy Ghost! This was soon followed by the awesome experience we have come to know as the Azusa Street Revival in 1906. From there, it swept like a prairie fire, filling the spiritually hungry souls with this wonderful prelude to the new heavens and new earth spoken of in Isaiah 65.

These last two verses of Isaiah 65 bring a smile to the face as we think about the great change occurring in heaven and earth: "I will answer their prayers before they finish praying. Wolves and lambs will graze together; lions and oxen will feed on straw. Snakes will eat only dirt! They won't bite or harm anyone on my holy mountain. I, the LORD, have spoken! (Isaiah 65:24–25). All this may be a millennium away; but with God, it will seem only as a day! May you live to a ripe old age.

"Reverend! Freeze!"

Beware that thou forget not the LORD thy God, in not keeping his commandments, and his judgments, and his statutes, which I command thee this day: Lest *when* thou hast eaten and art full, and hast built goodly houses, and dwelt *therein;* And *when* thy herds and thy flocks multiply, and thy silver and thy gold is multiplied, and all that thou hast is multiplied; Then thine heart be lifted up, and thou forget the LORD thy God, which brought thee forth out of the land of Egypt, from the house of bondage; Who led thee through that great and terrible wilderness, *wherein were fiery serpents*, and scorpions, and drought, where *there was* no water; who brought thee forth water out of the rock of flint; Who fed thee in the wilderness with manna, which thy fathers knew not, that he might humble thee, and that he might prove thee, to do thee good at thy latter end; And thou say in thine heart, My power and the might of *mine* hand hath gotten me this wealth. But thou shalt remember the LORD thy God: for *it is* he that giveth thee power to get wealth, that he may establish his covenant which he sware unto thy fathers, as *it is* this day.

—Deuteronomy 8:11–18

I'm not so sure that there is an exact duplication in scripture for the word rattlesnake. Suffice it to be close enough with the biblical terminology of fiery serpents. My understanding is that the term fiery has to do with the inflamed sting of its bite as well as the feeling of fire in the body because of it. "And the LORD sent fiery serpents among the people, and they bit the people; and much people of Israel died. Therefore the people came to Moses, and said, We have sinned, for we have spoken against the LORD, and against thee; pray unto the LORD, that he take away the serpents from us. And Moses prayed for the people. And the LORD said unto Moses, Make thee a fiery serpent, and set it upon a pole: and it shall come to pass, that every one that is bitten, when he looketh upon it, shall live. And Moses made a serpent of brass, and put it upon a pole, and it came to pass, that if a serpent had bitten any man, when he beheld the serpent of brass, he lived" (Numbers 21:6–9).

In 1970, I was pastoring my first church at the ripe old age of twenty-five years. I was the youngest adult man in the congregation, but there were several teenage boys. In that first summer of my pastoring, although I did not need to work on a secular job, I chose to work occasionally for one of the men in the church who owned a landscaping supply business. With trucks, bulldozers, and five or six of these young boys, we would salvage large crossties from the railroad between Santa Barbara and San Luis Obispo, California. I earned good money while also managing to have really good influence of time with those young guys.

The work was hard and dirty; and usually, it was very hot. Those crosstie beams were nine feet long and eight by ten inches and creosoted. All we had to do was pick up one end, stand it upright, let it down upon our shoulder, and walk with it to the truck—all 115 pounds of it. Did I mention hard, dirty, and heavy? Of course, with a bunch of young guys, as you might expect, we had a blast. Singing, lots of laughter, talking about church, and whatever else would help us work the day through.

One day, I learned a valuable lesson (right in front of those boys). It was a lesson about absolute and complete obedience. I was talking with one of the guys as I was lifting that heavy timber to stand it up and bring it onto my shoulder when the man, who was the boss, shouted, "Reverend, freeze!" Well what would you do? I froze. Then Bill pushed by me swiftly, stamping down hard with his booted foot, killing the rattlesnake that was already coiled to strike. Then he spoke to all of us a valuable lesson, "Reverend, you're my Pastor, but you can be bitten by a rattler just like anyone else. I'm really glad you obeyed me instantly. Talk and enjoy the fellowship, but keep your eyes open. There's snakes around here."

I was glad I obeyed him instantly without question. I don't think that snake noticed I was the Pastor at all. My official position didn't impress him one little bit. I kept my eyes open from then on and probably did less talking.

It Is High Time

And that, knowing the time, that now it is high time to awake out of sleep: for now is our salvation nearer than when we believed. The night is far spent, the day is at hand: let us therefore cast off the works of darkness, and let us put on the armour of light.

—Romans 13:11–12

And knowing the time that now it is high time to awake out of sleep. Can you not hear the call? It is a call to awake because it is high time (past the appropriate time to be doing). The night of unbelief is past. The day of salvation is at hand.

The call is one of duty. There is much to be done in His kingdom and in the saving of our own souls. The time is short. *Time is closing in upon us*; or as we might say, the time is pressed together. It is being squeezed into a narrower compass, like a sponge in a strong hand. There is an old story of a prisoner in a cell with contractile walls (one of the walls which squeezes together). Day by day his space lessens. Nearer and nearer, the walls are drawn together till they meet and crush him between them. So the walls of our time are closing in upon us.

Indolence and laziness must never be part of the Christian's life. My family and I arrived home at 2:00 a.m. after a long drive home from a Conference. My phone rang shortly after 5:00 a.m.! It was alias Moe! Now I've written previously about a good group of young boys in my first church to Pastor. One was this fellow who went by the name of alias Moe. Oh yes! He was never introduced without the additive "alias Moe."

"Why are you calling me so early, Moe?"

"Well," he said, "my clock is across the room, and I can't see it. And I need to know what time it is, and I didn't want to get up to look. So I called you."

Uh-huh! Mr. alias Moe was awarded a free trip to the Pastor's office for some personal attention about time and other things!

John Bunyan in Pilgrim's Progress told us "that when Hopeful came to a certain country, he began to be very dull and heavy of sleep. Wherefore he said, 'Let us lie down here and take one nap.' 'By no means,' said the other, 'lest sleeping, we wake no more.' 'Why, my brother? Sleep is sweet to the labouring man; we may be refreshed if we take a nap.' 'Do you not remember,' said the other, ' that one of the shepherds bid us beware of the Enchanted Ground? He meant by that, that we should beware of sleeping.' Therefore let us not sleep, as do others; but let us watch and be sober."

Slumbering and backsliding are closely allied. "Yet a little sleep, a little slumber, a little folding of the hands to sleep: So shall thy poverty come as one that travelleth; and thy want as an armed man" (Proverbs 24:33–34).

Here we are, citizens of the end-time, with a clock louder than Big Ben in London booming out across the world, bidding everyone to awake. The night is far spent, the day is at hand. Now is our salvation nearer than when we believed. It won't be long, 'til Jesus comes. I've never been to heaven, but I know I'll feel at home.

Invisible Hands

And in the fourth watch of the night Jesus went unto them, walking on the sea. And when the disciples saw him walking on the sea, they were troubled, saying, It is a spirit; and they cried out for fear. But straightway Jesus spake unto them, saying, Be of good cheer; it is I; be not afraid. And Peter answered him and said, Lord, if it be thou, bid me come unto thee on the water. And he said, Come. And when Peter was come down out of the ship, he walked on the water, to go to Jesus. But when he saw the wind boisterous, he was afraid; and beginning to sink, he cried, saying, Lord, save me. And immediately Jesus stretched forth *his* hand, and caught him, and said unto him, O thou of little faith, wherefore didst thou doubt?

—Matthew 14:25–31

As the preacher spoke last night, he mentioned our precious Phyllis who had only recently gone to be with the Lord. He made mention of her unusually strong grip. He correctly stated, "When she got hold of your hand to pray for you, she didn't let go." *Boom*! My mind went racing along the path he had just opened. How strong is the hand of Jesus? When your burden is too heavy for you to bear, can He hold you up? Will He grow weary and let you drop? Bits and pieces of song came to mind. Stuart Hamblen wrote, "Why I strayed from all his goodness, My poor mind can't understand. I'm to blame for my misfortune, I lost hold of his hands. Those hands that gave me mercy; When I'm wrong as wrong can be, If they really gave me justice, I'd be lost on a homeless sea."

Johnny Cash sang, "Once my soul was astray from the Heavenly Way; I was wretched and as vile as could be. But my Savior in love, gave me peace from above When He reached down His hand for me." And George Matheson gave such glorious expression when he penned the classic, "O Love, that will not let me go; I rest my weary soul in Thee; I give Thee back the life I owe That in Thine ocean depths its flow may richer, fuller be."

There I stood beside twenty-four-year-old Alice's bed; it was my very first "official" hospital visit as a twenty-six-year-old Pastor. That was fifty years ago! A childhood disease had left her with a physical impairment in her body so that walking and talking both were very difficult for her. After struggling through the talking portion of my visit, I informed Alice I would pray for her. Taking her by the hand, I began my prayer. I noticed she had quite a strong grip. And after my prayer was through, and I had said Amen! she continued to hold my hand tightly. I said it again, "Amen!" and again, "Amen!" Finally, in desperation, I gently said, "Alice, you can let go of my hand, now."

In her halting, somewhat slurred speech, she said, "I-I-I c—I can't!"

I didn't know she had little or no motor control in her hands. So one by one, I pried her fingers loose until her hand let go, and I was free!

From time to time, I am wont to burst out singing, "Jesus, hold my hand. I need Thee every hour. Through this pilgrim land, protect me by Thy power. Hear my feeble plea. O Lord, look down on me. When I kneel in prayer, I hope to meet You there. Blessed Jesus, hold my hand."

I have just returned from an early morning breakfast appointment. Here on my desk is a note written by my sweet wife. Apparently, she awakened and came into my office and read the unfinished document. So from her own heart are these very appropriate words to finish this devotion: "Invisible hands are waiting to guide you; Invisible hands are always beside you; So, pray and believe and help you'll receive from invisible hands."

Never discount the power of strong hands.

The Black Racer

Wherefore I put thee in remembrance that thou stir up the gift of God, which is in thee by the putting on of my hands. For God hath not given us the spirit of fear; but of power, and of love, and of a sound mind.

—2 Timothy 1:6–7

There was a boy growing up in the country who had heard scary stories about a snake called a Black Racer. He had heard that it would chase you. These stories kept him very alert as he walked up and down the gravel roads around where he lived. One day, his Mom asked him to go to the neighbor's house and borrow an iron because hers was broken.

He started up the road casting a watchful eye to each side of the road where the weeds were grown up along the way. He could just imagine one of those Black Racers lying back in the shadows just waiting to slip up on him and bite him. He borrowed the iron and started back down the road toward home when he sensed something was following him. He looked over his shoulder, and sure enough, there in the road behind him was a snake just raising up to bite him. He took off with all the speed of an Olympic contestant, running nearly all the way home until it seemed he would not be able to breath any longer. Fearfully, he looked over his shoulder to see if the Black Racer was still there; and there, to his amazement, was the iron cord dragging on the ground behind him. He had almost ran himself to death running from an iron cord.

How often do we run from things in the same way just because we haven't looked at them from the right perspective? Not to be forgotten was the night I was awakened as a small boy, afraid and terrified in the darkness of my room. As I lay sobbing, Mother called to me, "France, what's wrong?"

"Someone is looking in my room," I answered. "They keep waving their arms, and they're wearing a big hat. Momma, I'm scared."

With that, Mother turned on the light and showed me her large sweater hanging in the hallway, along with her large hat she wore to protect her from the hot California sun. The wind was blowing the sweater, causing it to move as though it was "waving its arms."

Oh, how the enemy loves to play tricks with our minds. I say "the enemy" because "God hath not given us the spirit of fear; but of power, and of love, and of a sound mind" (2 Timothy 1:7). And by the way, Black Racers can take on many different forms in our minds. "They're talking about me." "They were laughing at me." "They don't want me." "I'm not as good as they are." And don't you make any mistake about it. Those Black Racers are fast, and they can really bite!

So the next time you see somebody waving their arms at you (especially if they have on a big hat) or if you need to borrow an iron, just remember, God did not give you the spirit of fear. And there isn't any Black Racer, real or otherwise, can ever defeat God's protecting power. You just need to see him in the right perspective (i.e., as a defeated foe).

And the God of peace shall bruise Satan under your feet shortly. (Romans 16:20)

Extraordinary Times

In my efforts to present a Pastor's Devotion, I have made every attempt to use my own material, in part or in whole. Today, it seems appropriate to present an excerpt of the Deerfield Honor Society induction speech written by Helen Crowley, a teacher at Deerfield High School. I have not changed it at all.

July 26, 2017

> We are, indeed, living in extraordinary times, when the very existence of fact is challenged, and people are questioning the institutions we depend on. So, what I say to you matters—if only in the sense that I try to speak honestly and with integrity about what I believe to be true.
>
> I wake up each morning with incredible responsibilities: a responsibility to keep those under my charge safe and healthy, to love and care, to promote kindness, and, above all, a responsibility to instill ethics and morals. I emphasize this idea of ethics and morals because it is not something to be taken lightly. It is these attributes that dictate our daily actions...that guide us to ultimately be who we are and what we will become.
>
> I have come to learn that we must condition our ethical self—like anything else. As a Track athlete, we run repeat 400s and distance training. As a musician, we rehearse for our concerts

and performances, perhaps playing the same few songs over and over again. I've come to notice that we emphasize strengthening our talents and passions, often forgetting to strengthen the foundation of who we are.

Wintley Phipps said, "It is in the quiet crucible of your personal private sufferings that your noblest dreams are born, and God's greatest gifts are given in compensation for what you've been through."

It is our mission to cultivate the ethical being inside of each one of our students. We urge our Youth to stand up for what you believe is right, even if you are standing alone.

It is often in the face of adversity or conflict that our ethical self is questioned: Do we do what we know is right or do we act against this inner voice? We work hard at encouraging our Youth to act by what they know to be right, to be moral, to be ethical.

While we recognize that this strengthening takes time and patience, we believe our youth will be more prepared for these "Extraordinary Times" in which we live.

Extraordinary times... Yes. But to conclude, however, Vance Havner stated, "We have no business living ordinary lives in such extraordinary times." (Helen Crowley)

Thank God for an educator of such high ethics and integrity who stands daily to lead our children in paths of righteousness (FWM).

The Law of the Garbage Truck

I came across this little piece of homespun advice while browsing through some of my "Possibility" files. I noticed it had been sent to me from Ruby Isaksson, who had recently gone to be with the Lord. I doubt she ever was in a taxicab or New York City for that matter, but the content of this article gathered from "who knows where" certainly aligns with her spirit and happy smile she gave to the world. I hope you will enjoy the story.

How often do you let other people's nonsense change your mood? Do you let a bad driver, rude waiter, curt boss, or an insensitive employee ruin your day? For an instant, you're probably set back on your heels. However, the mark of a successful person is how quickly she can get back her focus on what's important.

Here is a bit of philosophy I learned in the back of a New York City taxicab. Here's what happened:

I hopped in a taxi, and we took off for Grand Central Station. We were driving in the right lane when, suddenly, a black car jumped out of a parking space right in front of us. My taxi driver slammed on his brakes, skidded, and missed the other car's back end by just inches! The driver of the other car, the guy who almost caused a big accident, whipped his head around and started yelling bad words at us. My taxi driver just smiled and waved at the guy. I mean, he was genuinely friendly.

So, I said, "Why did you just do that? This guy almost ruined your car and sent us to the hospital!" And this is when my taxi driver told me what I now call "The Law of the Garbage Truck."

"Many people are like garbage trucks. They run around full of garbage, full of frustration, full of anger, and full of disappointment. As their garbage piles up, they need a place to dump it. And if you let them, they'll dump it on you. When someone wants to dump on you, don't take it personally. You just smile, wave, wish them well, and move on. You'll be happy you did."

So this was it, The Law of the Garbage Truck. I started thinking, *How often do I let garbage trucks run right over me? And how often do I take their garbage and spread it to other people at work, at home, on the streets?* It was that day I said, "I'm not going to do it anymore."

I began to see garbage trucks. I see the load they're carrying. I see them coming to drop it off. And like my taxi driver, I don't make it a personal thing; I just smile, wave, wish them well, and I move on. Successful people do not let garbage trucks take over their day.

What about you? What would happen in your life, starting today, if you let more garbage trucks pass you by? Here's what I think: I think you'll be happier. Life's too short to wake up in the morning with regrets, so love the people who treat you right. Say a quick prayer for the ones who don't. Believe that everything happens for a reason.

If you get a chance, *take it*! If it changes your life, *let it*! Nobody said it would be easy. But it's a sure thing; it'll be worth it!

Don't Lose Your Keys

Ask, and it shall be given you; seek, and ye shall find; knock, and it shall be opened unto you: For everyone that asketh receiveth; and he that seeketh findeth; and to him that knocketh it shall be opened.

—Matthew 7:7–8

A key is a strange-looking object, usually made of brass for its hardness and ability to withstand somewhat abusive use—twisting, turning, sometimes under great pressure. Yet, for the most part, they do not break. Many years ago, keys were large, sometimes six to eight inches in length, made of cast iron, and very heavy. Over the years, keys were made smaller until they are now usually about two inches in length and much easier to carry in one's pocket than hefting about a ring of keys weighing two or three pounds. But with the convenience of the smaller size also comes the greater risk of losing those small keys.

Take, for instance, this past week. With a change of residence coming up in about three weeks, my wife and I have begun the process of gathering our "stuff" together, stuff like our "important" papers and documents, etc. It happens that this current house has a small security box built into the wall system. It seems quite secure and can be opened with a special key, which I could not find. After a time of confession made to my wife about a missing key, we both continued to look for that key for several days. Now let me present a scriptural side to this story about missing keys.

James said, "Ye lust, and have not: ye kill, and desire to have, and cannot obtain: ye fight and war, yet ye have not, because ye ask not. Ye ask, and receive not, because ye ask amiss, that ye may consume it upon your lusts" (James 4:2–3). As I am writing just now, I thought to only print the pertinent statement here about asking and receiving. But as the scripture hung suspended upon my computer screen, it seemed to present so many aspects of our conflicting emotions. These emotions are reflections of what is going on in our hearts and minds as we grapple with the knowledge that there are missing parts to our lives. We want the treasures hidden away "somewhere," but where (and what) is the key?

We are filled with lust, but we still have not. We desire to have, but we cannot obtain—often, I dare say—because we are too impatient. We get involved in fights and quarrels, which occasionally escalate into wars with those within our circle of loved ones. And when the dust settles, we pause and look around, taking inventory, and must admit we still don't have what we were looking for. Why? Because we don't ask, or because our asking is based on wrong motives. Usually, because we want to satisfy our lusts, so the circle is complete, and we are back where we started. "Ye lust, and have not."

So (going back to the missing key) over a period of four or five days, I prayed, admittedly a couple of rather anemic little prayers, asking God to help me find that key. I went to the admin office within our strata, asking for a possible duplicate key. Did I mention it was a special key, like round, not flat? The lady even gave me a ring full of those little creatures.

"See, if any of these will work!"

Not a chance. But I could hear my wife praying with sincerity and frequency, "Oh, Lord! We need to find that key! Help us, God."

As we lay down in bed last night, I heard her say pray again, "Oh, Lord, please help us find that key." Suddenly, I had a vague memory of putting it in a certain place. I told my wife. *Click*! On came the bedside lamp.

"What are you doing," I asked.

"I'm going to look for the key."

"Let's look in the morning."

"No," she said. "I believe I know where you placed it!" Her determination created excitement in me, for I also began to remember. I got up and joined her in the search. We found the key! Holding hands, we rejoiced and praised God for answered prayer! Ask, and you shall receive.

The Tabernacle of a Thousand Days

How amiable are thy tabernacles, O LORD of
hosts! My soul longeth, yea, even fainteth for
the courts of the LORD: my heart and my flesh
crieth out for the living God. Yea, the sparrow
hath found an house, and the swallow a nest for
herself, where she may lay her young, even thine
altars, O LORD of hosts, my King, and my God.
Blessed are they that dwell in thy house: they will
be still praising thee. Selah.

Blessed is the man whose strength is in thee;
in whose heart are the ways of them (those who
dwell in thy house). Who passing through the
valley of Baca make it a well; the rain also fil-
leth the pools. They go from strength to strength,
every one of them in Zion appeareth before God.
O LORD God of hosts, hear my prayer: give ear,
O God of Jacob. Selah.

Behold, O God our shield, and look upon
the face of thine anointed. For a day in thy courts
is better than a thousand. I had rather be a door-
keeper in the house of my God, than to dwell
in the tents of wickedness. For the LORD God is
a sun and shield: the LORD will give grace and
glory: no good thing will he withhold from them

that walk uprightly. O LORD of hosts, blessed is
the man that trusteth in thee.

—Psalm 84:1–12

The good man loves the house of God—

1. Because it is a constant testimony for God in the midst of
   a crooked and perverse generation;
2. Because it is a refuge to him from the ungodly and unholy
   elements of a sinful world;
3. Because it is a school in which he becomes more fully
   instructed in the truth as it is in Jesus;
4. Because it is the home where he enjoys the communion of
   saints;
5. Because there he enjoys fellowship with the Heavenly
   Father;
6. Because it identifies him more and more with the paradise
   of God above.

Think about this next time you feel too tired and weary for yet
another church service.

One day spent in your house, this beautiful place
of worship, beats thousands spent on Greek island
beaches. I'd rather scrub floors in the house of my
God than be honored as a guest in the palace of
sin. (Psalm 84:10 MSG)

Not only are they blessed whose home is in the sanctuary (spiritually speaking) and who spend their days in perpetual praise; but
those also are blessed who, though at a distance, have God for their
strength and help and press on in pursuit of growing yet further in
His presence.

Though they (whose home is in the sanctuary) encounter difficulties, they are still blessed. Though they encounter difficulties, they

shall, with increasing strength, pursue His way until they reach their blessed destiny. In contemplation of the privileges to be enjoyed both here and there, the one who dwells in the sanctuary of the Most High prays. He invokes the help of the Almighty. He seeks the favor of God in the pursuits and issues of import in his life. Constantly appearing before His throne in prayerful supplication, he uses wonderful titles of honor and praise: "the Almighty," "O Lord God of Hosts," "O God of Jacob," "O God, our shield." And these are rightly spoken, for our God is an awesome God, worthy of such exalted praise!

The Storm of Ephesus

On our Mediterranean Cruise for our fiftieth wedding anniversary, Gloria and I encountered a major disappointment. Our plans called for an all-day stop at the biblical town of Ephesus. Our friend, Evangeline Rodenbush, spoke enthusiastically of the wonder of historical significance associated with this part of our itinerary. We were very excited about it.

Soon after we had departed from Istanbul, however, we heard the captain's voice coming over the ship's PA system, advising us that, "Unfortunately, because of a storm in the area, we will not be stopping at Ephesus because of the possible dangers involved in docking and disembarking for the shore excursions."

We were so disappointed. Because of Gloria's knee surgeries, she was unable to do a lot of walking on those shore excursions. For this one, we had made special arrangements for taxis and wheelchairs, hoping to participate in this excursion, which, for us, would have such special meaning. We really hoped to do this. But it was not to be.

The captain's decision was made to preserve the safety of the ship, the crew, and all passengers aboard. There was a storm that night. Oh, how that ship was buffeted by the wind and waves. We sailed right on past Ephesus. But we were safe. There was a purpose greater than our desires. We could have complained. We could have done several things but to no purpose or satisfaction. Instead, we put the port of Ephesus behind us and sailed on to the next port of call, Venice.

It has been my experience in life that from time to time, storms will unexpectedly interrupt and alter one's plans. Four of our granddaughters (with our beautiful great-grands) live in Florida.

I've noticed there is a lot of activity whenever "storm warnings" are issued: Cases of bottled water and nonperishable food is purchased; retail and commercial businesses have plywood panels installed covering their windows. You know what I'm talking about. You've seen it as well. It is called "Preparing for the Storm!" And the storm hits. Phenomenal winds, rain, trees blowing over, signs and billboards sailing through the air, destruction, and chaos (with not a few of us saying, "I'm glad we're not there!").

Then something amazing and wonderful happens. The storm passes. Moves on. It's over! And the most amazing and awesome part of all is you begin to see these people back in business. Restaurants open again. Traffic is moving. People are going to work. The family calls and says, "We're okay. Our phone service was blown out for a few days, but we were okay! God had His hand upon us! And sighs of relief all around could be heard. People were saying, "Boy! That was some storm! But we made it. Thank God!"

Such is life! No matter how terrible the storm, God is greater; and eventually all storms cease.

Unforgettable

The month of September is a notoriously busy month for the Masons. Several September birthdays have their mark on the calendar (including one for yours truly). I always think of my beautiful mother-in-law on September 10 (God rest her soul). Two or three greats get in on the candle club as well, plus at least one wedding anniversary. For many years, we have also inevitably had to work General Conference attendance into the September itinerary as well. But with personal significance is September 13, 14, and 15.

We were having Revival services in the old Mt. Zion Tabernacle in Goshen, California. Pastor James Barnett and Evangelist Ted Molander were leading the church in a search for a move of God. Things were happening. At one noonday, a little girl had drunk some Clorox bleach. And with no evidence of breathing or heartbeat when she was found by her father, he rushed her about two miles to the church. Bursting into the church, he found the evangelist in prayer who, seeing the situation, laid his hands on the child in Jesus Name, and she immediately began breathing and crying.

Such was the atmosphere of miracles in our home church in the week of September 14, 1963. God was dealing with my heart so strongly, seeming to want me to come closer to Him to surrender my life to him more completely. I had already heard what I thought was a voice urging me to give myself to ministry. Doubt flung itself about my mind, filling my thoughts with confusion and fear. I had asked Bro. Molander what it was all about. Thank God for wise counsel. "Just keep listening with much prayer. If it truly was God, and you are not rejecting Him, He will speak again." (Remember the young boy, Samuel!)

And He did. During the altar service on Thursday night, while praying with someone else, suddenly, I was in a trance, seeing a vision. It was very much like seeing a video inside my head. I could hear everything else that was going on, but it was not commanding my attention. What I was seeing in the Spirit did have my attention. I saw myself standing just a few feet up on a very tall and long stairway, looking out over a huge mass of people. They were crying, reaching up their hands, shouting for help. It was a crowd of people who were urgent about being helped. Standing next to me on the stairs was a person whom I simply knew was Jesus. I did not see His face but rather his form, his body. I said to Him, "What do I do? These people need help."

The Lord said, "Watch me. Do like I do." And reaching down His hand into the mass of people, He took someone by the hand and lifted them up onto the stairway, and they started climbing. "Now, you try it," Jesus said.

I will never forget the feeling of such hope from the people and the compassion in my heart as I reached down my hand and took a hand that was urgently grasping for mine. I managed to lift them onto the stairway, and they began to climb higher.

I was nineteen years old. The day before was my birthday; the next day was to be our very first wedding anniversary. I could tell much more of that night of vision and calling but suffice to say that I, too, once was among that multitude—lost, hoping, needing someone to help me. When He reached down His hand for me, I was lost and undone. But He made me His Son. When He reached down His hand for me.

The Good Old Days?

I am amazed how things have changed in my lifetime. Listening to a conversation my wife was having with one of our granddaughters yesterday, I could feel the excitement as she talked about just being hired for a new job, working for a large corporate firm. When inquiry was made about pay, the excitement level went even higher.

"Nana, I'll be working at home, and the pay will be over $20 per hour!"

Now I have a minor problem with dizziness, but that really had my head spinning. That being our anniversary day, my mind raced backward to our wedding day. Yep, I worked until 2:00 p.m. then took off three hours early to prepare for our wedding. I knew my paycheck would be short because, after all, I'd forfeited three hours of work. And at $1.25 per hour, that was going to make a difference. Thankfully, Mr. Edmiston gave me a 25¢ raise (and a toaster) as a wedding gift. That would help greatly to pay for our $35 per month honeymoon cottage!

My father put a great work ethic into his four sons. When he was just a young man himself, with a wife and small family to care for, he contracted to make cross ties for the railroad. He would cut down the trees, saw them (by hand—no Stihl chain saws in those days) to nine feet long; then with an axe, he would hew them (by hand) into an eight-by-ten-inch railroad crosstie. And he was paid 50¢ for each one he made. He could average about six or eight per day.

After the war was over (World War II—Pearl Harbor, Hitler, etc.) Dad and Mom decided they could do better if they moved to California. And they did do better. O.J. went to work on a farm, making 90¢ an hour. But it was steady work, which helped a lot during the winter months. Nancy (or Viola, as she was known then) worked seasonally, packing peaches and plums for the New York market, usually being paid about 5¢ for each box packed. After the fruit season was over, she would work in the cotton fields, chopping (thinning) the baby plants and cutting out the weeds—hard, hot work. But she was paid the going rate of 90¢ an hour.

Before leaving Oklahoma to move to California, Mother and Dad both became involved in a small Pentecostal Church where services were being held by Bro. Charlie Sprinkles in the schoolhouse located on Yeller Hammer Mountain. The old schoolhouse has not survived, but the experience of their baptism in the Holy Ghost did. Although they both were young in Christ, my great-grandmother Mammy Box insured their spirituality was secure when they left for out of state. When they arrived in California, their intentions were to stop in Bakersfield, but they had heard about a church in Goshen where services were being held in a chicken house. The saints had cleaned out the feathers and everything else and found they could accommodate about thirty people. And the Holy Ghost began to move. There are many details to be talked about, but suffice it to say that regardless of the environment, origins, or the place, when there are people hungry for God, He will provide the agenda. God helped those folks establish a church in the heart of the San Joaquin Valley, which is today one of the strong, thriving congregations of California. From those humble beginnings have come several ministers who dedicated themselves to the preaching of the gospel.

Far and wide, people knew of O.J. and Nancy Mason. They knew of them being very kind and helpful to their neighbors. They knew they were deeply religious and committed to the Pentecostal experience and lifestyle. Poor people, doctors, business owners alike were touched by their lives. I am so deeply grateful for this faithful man and woman who never once faltered in living for God even in the Good Old Days.

God bless the memory of my Mother and Father.

Pilfering the Cache

Well here we were—moving day! The legal work was all completed yesterday afternoon, and the realtor immediately was at our door with new keys, pronouncing those marvelous words, "It's yours! You can move in." So according to plan, we immediately loaded our beds in the moving truck to avoid the predicted heavy rains. After delivering them to our new home (and taking them upstairs. *Ugh*!), it was late. We were tired and just a bit unsure of sleeping the first night in an empty house with nothing but beds. I mean, what if we woke up with the midnight munchies, or we just wanted to sit in the dark and talk, where would we sit? Anyway, we stayed one last night in our good old house—tried, trusted, and totally packed into boxes. She slept on the big comfortable couch; I slept on a little, tiny mattress taken from a hide-a-bed love seat. Did I say lumpy and narrow?

At 4:50 in the morning, I waved a white flag and surrendered the war of fighting for sleep and got up. After a quick trip down the hall, I had only one thing on my mind—*coffee*! In the kitchen, aah! there was my faithful Keurig, ready to go. But where was my coffee? Oh *no*! It was packed away in a box, neat and tidy and even labeled properly: *Coffee Cups, Etc.*! It was that *etc.!* that I was interested in. Packed away! Who did that?

Well I got a sharp knife and moved quietly. I mustn't wake up the one enjoying sleeping on the big comfortable couch. After all, she didn't drink coffee. She wouldn't understand cutting open the box. "It's already packed! Oh, for heaven's sake, grow up! Drink a glass of water. It's good for you." See what I mean?

So with a wonderful cup of hot coffee in hand, I found my computer and began to write while I contentedly sipped. My first thought from the keyboard was, *Mason, do you call this nonsense a devotion? What is so devoted about the Pastor pilfering coffee from a moving box at 5:00 a.m.?* Well, it goes like this—and I must ask you to be willing to forbear with me as I ask Mr. Peterson to allow us to use his translation of the Bible called The Message one more time— here goes:

> True, God made everything beautiful in itself and in its time—but he's left us in the dark, so we can never know what God is up to, whether he's coming or going. I've decided that there's nothing better to do than go ahead and have a good time and get the most we can out of life. That's it—eat, drink, and make the most of your job. It's God's gift. (Ecclesiastes 3:11–13)

This text does not tell us to sin. It says God made everything beautiful in its time. It says that we often do not know what God is up to. And like the song says, "I just feel like something good is about to happen. I just feel like something good is on its way. He has promised that He'd open all of heaven. And, brother, it could happen any day."

So, friends, go ahead and have a cup of coffee or tea or Diet Coke or a glass of water. This is the day that the Lord has made. Rejoice and be glad in it. (Boy, am I ever glad I found the cache of *etc.!*)

Time Is Filled with Swift Transition

Packing boxes were scattered here and there throughout our newly acquired house. These boxes were filled with kitchen utensils, pots, and pans. Dishes were there also. That room had books, and those boxes over there were filled with books also. We were blessed with books—Pastor's library, you know. And of course, her cookbooks! Not all the boxes were filled with books. Several boxes had the usual items that make for a comfortable home, items of purpose and use, and otherwise. Did I mention clocks?

Unpacking is not an easy task. Nor do the boxes get emptied quickly. This fact was evident to me this morning as I lay on the couch, hoping to catch a few more minutes of sleep. The house was still and quiet. Suddenly, I became acutely aware of a highly annoying and obnoxious sound: *ticktock, ticktock, ticktock*. I was equally aware of what the source of the annoyance was. *Ticktock, ticktock, ticktock*. Have you ever noticed how you begin to mentally match the cadence of a ticking clock to other rhythmic sounds, like your breathing or your heartbeat? Now that one will really get you going! "Why is my heart doing the offbeat of the clock? *Tick* thump *tock*; *tick* thump *tock*; *tick* thump *tock*; *tick* thump *tock*—man, this is crazy! I shouldn't have had that cup of coffee so early in the morning."

By now a part of a song was stuck in my head: "Time is filled up and…nope. Transit time is…nope. Time full of—wait, here we go. Time is filled with swift transition. What's the rest of it? I'll just lie here a minute longer. It'll come to me." And so, the remedy was to get up and find the *ticktock* box and move it or find the clock and remove the battery or…or employ the repeated phrase in each of these options. *Get up. Ticktock, ticktock, ticktock.* After holding a mental conference with myself, it was decided that getting up was the better part of valor. I got up.

And the song did come to me. And after googling the lyrics, it began to speak to me, "Open your heart and let the words speak to you too."

Hold to God's Unchanging Hand

Time is filled with swift transition,
Naught of earth unmoved can stand,
Build your hope on things eternal;
Hold to God's unchanging hand.

Trust in Him who will not leave you.
Whatso'er the years may bring,
When your earthly friends forsake you,
Still more closely to Him cling.

Hold to God's unchanging hand. Hold to God's unchanging hand. Build your hopes on things eternal; And hold to God's unchanging hand.

Modern-Day Miracles

Therefore we ought to give the more earnest heed to the things which we have heard, lest at any time we should let them slip.

—Hebrews 2:1

Our own brother in fellowship, the late Dr. Marvin Treece, accurately described our comprehension of this truth as a ship slipping past the harbor. This generation must deal with the issue that God's Word has been given as the means of our salvation. His Word is settled forever in the heavens. There are truths and significant events that have occurred that must not be allowed to "slip" away from us. Not only is written history important but perhaps even more so is the importance of history that is spoken, passed down from generation to generation.

I recall Bro. Charles Hopper, a member of our home church, was working on a ranch. One day, he discovered he had gone off to work and had forgotten his lunch. He decided to drive home to have lunch, something he never did. He and his wife had a sweet little girl who was born with Down Syndrome. When he arrived home for lunch, as he walked in the door, he found his daughter lying unconscious on the floor in the kitchen. Near her was a bottle of household bleach. He shouted, "My baby is dead!" And scooping her into his arms, he dashed out to his car.

Now the church was involved in Revival services at that time. He drove approximately two miles with his unconscious baby who was not breathing. It was shortly after 12:00 noon (his lunchtime). Bro Charles had driven to the church! Inexplicably, the evangelist was in the church, praying at lunchtime! The father rushed into the church with his baby and shouted to the evangelist, "My baby is dead!" The evangelist, already praying, simply laid his hand on the child in the Name of Jesus. Gasping and coughing, the little girl began struggling as she revived and went to her Daddy. Coincidence? The Bible would have us believe that God orchestrated the forgotten lunch of the dad and the evangelist having a prayer meeting at lunchtime in order to produce a life-saving miracle!

> And we know that all things work together for good to them that love God, to them who are the called according to his purpose. (Romans 8:28)

Tunie Mayes was a quiet and soft-spoken beautiful First Nation Christian lady. She was a woman of prayer who lived across the street from the church. She often could be found in the Prayer Room, day or night, quietly praying. One Sunday night, after a day spent in the House of God, she was awakened from her sleep about 1:15 a.m. She quietly began to pray as she lay in bed but felt hot, so she pushed her window open to let a cool breeze into the room. Also, she sat up in the corner of her bed with her feet tucked up under her.

Suddenly, there was the sound of screeching tires and sirens, and her house was violently shaken with a terrible crash. The front of a large pickup truck was on top of the foot of her bed, spewing steam out of the engine. Instantly, with catlike reflexes, that seventy-six-year-old lady leapt out her opened window and escaped, unharmed. But the danger was not yet over. The truck was also sitting on top of the large gas meter attached to the house, and the motor was extremely hot!

Sis. Tunie later told me, "Pastor, I was so tired from being in church all day. I didn't understand why God woke me up after midnight to pray. And I just never sit up with my feet tucked under me like that. And, Pastor, I just seemed to fly out of that window with no effort. But when I look at my house with all the damage (the house was knocked six inches off the foundation), I know why now. It was a miracle from God that I'm alive." Amen!

These events happened. There has been no embellishment, no exaggeration. Repeating a statement from above, these are truths and significant events that have occurred that must not be allowed to "slip" away from us.

> God also bearing them witness, both with signs
> and wonders, and with divers miracles, and gifts
> of the Holy Ghost, according to his own will.
> (Hebrews 2:4)

God still works miracles! And what He's done for others, He'll do for you! Trust Him.

Does God Care What We Do to Each Other?

In Mark's gospel narrative, the focus of attention is upon Jesus in a small boat with his disciples. They were going across the Sea of Galilee to the country of the Gadarenes. Two potentially disastrous and wonderful situations awaited them. First, we have several men in a ship with Jesus headed into a storm. Secondly, in Gadara, we have a storm that had been raging within a man for a long time. Perhaps you will find yourself somewhere in this story from Mark 4 and 5.

The Man in a Storm, or the Storm in a Man—this defines most all of us with our own personal life issues. It is the man asleep on a pillow in the hinder part of the ship who determines the outcomes for both categories of people. A primary observation is made here. When Jesus and His group of disciples departed for the other side, "there were also with him other little ships." Jesus had many who followed Him and, yes, for many different reasons. The point to be made is when Jesus arose from sleeping (as a weary man) and rebuked the wind (as the Master of creation) and said unto the sea, "Peace, be still," the wind ceased, and there was a great calm. But notice! All the little ships benefitted from the calm!

As the wind was howling about them, the ship was pitching and bucking like a demented animal. And the specter of an impending grave in the depths of Galilee awaited them. The question was asked, "Master, carest thou not that we perish?" The answer, paraphrased in The Message, makes me want to laugh at the storm! "Awake now, he told the wind to pipe down and said to the sea, 'Quiet! Settle down!' The wind ran out of breath; the sea became smooth as glass." Does Jesus care?

Cain stood out in the field where he had just become the world's first murderer. Suddenly, there was a presence and a voice. "Cain, what have you done? Where is Abel? You are to care for your brother. The voice of thy brother's blood crieth unto me from the ground." Sin has a voice, which cries to God for vengeance as when the blood of Abel called for justice.

- From every bloody, murderous crime scene goes up a cry to God!
- From every bloody barroom brawl where lifeblood has been shed in a drunken stupor, there goes up a cry to God.
- From every school classroom burst in upon by shooters with death-wielding weapons, there goes up a cry to God.
- From every home where anger has erupted into the killing of a family member, there goes up a cry to God.
- From every bloody abortion clinic, there goes up a cry to God from the unborn who have no voice.
- From every gruesome "mercy" killing, there goes up a cry to God.
- From every assisted suicide contraption of poisons, there goes up a cry to God.
- From every hospital, nursing home, and center for the care of the elderly where the awful abomination of euthanasia is carried out by some misguided "caregiver," there goes up a cry to the Almighty God.

Does God even notice what's going on? Does He care? There are some who act as if God takes no note of what they are doing. Rest assured, not a single thing escapes His notice. He not only notes the actions of men but weighs them as well. Job agreed, for he said, "Doth not He see my ways, and count all my steps" (Job 31:4)?

Does Jesus care when my heart is pained?

Oh, yes, he cares. I know he cares too deeply for mirth or song.

His heart is touched with my grief as the burdens press, and the cares distress.

When the days are weary, the long nights dreary, and the way grows weary and long, I know my Savior cares.

God takes note of what is going on in the world, in your world. Whether the man is in the storm, or the storm is in the man, He cares!

Guilty as Charged...or Not!

Blessed is he whose transgression is forgiven, whose sin is covered. Blessed is the man unto whom the LORD imputeth not iniquity, and in whose spirit there is no guile. When I kept silence, my bones waxed old through my roaring all the day long. For day and night thy hand was heavy upon me: my moisture is turned into the drought of summer. Selah. I acknowledged my sin unto thee, and mine iniquity have I not hid. I said, I will confess my transgressions unto the LORD; and thou forgavest the iniquity of my sin. Selah.

—Psalm 32:1–5

Can you identify with a guilty king? He feels miserable and unhappy all day long. What is guilt?

Guilt is the fact or condition of having committed an offense, especially a willful violation of a legal or moral code. (The Reader's Digest Great Encyclopedic Dictionary)

This willful violation of moral integrity brings deep feelings of remorse. Let's look at why you feel guilty and what to do about it.

You may feel guilty because you are guilty. David felt guilty because of his sins. So let's admit that we are all guilty before God. Here are some selected statements found in Romans 3:10–23:

> As it is written, There is none righteous, no, not one: there is none that doeth good, no, not one. Destruction and misery are in their ways: And the way of peace have they not known: There is no fear of God before their eyes. For all have sinned, and come short of the glory of God. (Romans 3:10–25)

Like Belshazzar, we've been weighed and found wanting. But guilt feelings can have a positive effect. They are like the warning signs of cancer. They are like pains that warn of a serious problem. They may come from an awakened conscience or from the conviction of the Holy Spirit. However they may come, thank God for guilt feelings if they bring you to Him.

You may feel guilty because you have not been forgiven. Before confessing his sins and receiving forgiveness, David felt older than his years and that God was against him. In our text, he felt as though he was in a spiritual desert. But forgiveness was available to David, but he had not accepted it. We have an absolute guarantee of forgiveness from Almighty God.

> If we confess our sins, he is faithful and just to forgive us our sins, and to cleanse us from all unrighteousness. (1 John 1:9)

Our forgiveness depends on accepting God's gracious offer to sinners. Look at it again: "If we confess our sins, he is faithful and just to forgive us our sins." He is "faithful and just." But even grace does not force forgiveness on us. You can be free from guilt by accepting forgiveness.

Read and identify with the guilty king's confession.

> For I acknowledge my transgressions: and my sin is ever before me. Against thee, thee only, have I sinned, and done this evil in thy sight: that thou

mightest be justified when thou speakest, and be clear when thou judgest. (Psalm 51:3–4)

I acknowledged my sin unto thee, and mine iniquity have I not hid. I said, I will confess my transgressions unto the LORD; and thou forgavest the iniquity of my sin. (Psalm 32:3–4)

David sought and found forgiveness. David's confession of his sins fits us all. Sins confessed are sins forgiven. This will always be true. Why remain a prisoner of past sins? Bring your sins to the one who died for sinners. You do not have to feel guilty anymore. And with sins forgiven, "There is therefore now no condemnation to them which are in Christ Jesus!

The Width of the Boat

But when the morning was now come, Jesus stood on the shore: but the disciples knew not that it was Jesus. Then Jesus saith unto them, Children, have ye any meat? They answered him, No. And he said unto them, Cast the net on the right side of the ship, and ye shall find. They cast therefore, and now they were not able to draw it for the multitude of fishes.

—John 21:4–6

There are few scenes in the gospel more impressive than this in the early morning by the Sea of Galilee. The dreadful events of Calvary are past. The night of darkness is ended. Jesus is risen, and the strain of the insecurities of the future is over. There seems to be a universal question among the small band of fishermen friends: What do we do now? Peter said, "I go a-fishing."

A word of caution: There are leaders, and there are followers—some intentional, others unintentional. You may be one or the other. Assess the consequences of your role. So Peter and his comrades toiled all night; but for all their labor, their fishing was a failure. They toiled all night—nothing. I love the synchrony of words: morning—master. It was just at the dawning of the day, and Jesus stood by the lake and called out to them as they fished, "Children, have ye any meat?" A straight question can only receive a straight answer—it was No!

The figure on the seashore said, "Cast the net on the right side of the boat." He watched as they gathered it all together then turned from their usual left-handed position and cast the net from the right side, and it was quickly (and wondrously) filled with fish—153 to be exact! Instantly, John turned to his fishing partners, saying, "It is the Lord."

Stop. Go back into your thinking. What does it suggest to you? "Cast the net on the right side of the boat?" We are talking about the mere width of the boat. There are two or three items presented for your consideration.

First, what we long for is often nearer than we think.

Somehow, within the sweep of their net was exactly what they had been toiling for. They had cast the net repeatedly—nothing. They were tired. They had lost heart. They were weary, hungry, and hopeless. They may have felt that the ecological system of the lake had somehow changed. Someone might have said, "There's no fish here now, boys. Let's go home." But what they had been looking for all night was not far away.

Then, secondly, we should never be afraid to change our methods.

What a great success the fishermen would have missed if they sullenly refused to cast the net on the other side of the boat. At the voice of the Lord, they tried a new method, a new plan. With their obedience, everything became different from left to right, from monotonous methods to a new technique, from nothing to a boat suddenly in danger of sinking because of the great result of following the voice of the one on the shore.

Finally, just a brief comment—brief but oh so important. Christ can manage our business better than we can ourselves. The Lord can give advice to the most astute business person. Consult him when all your labor seems in vain. Go to him before every new venture, asking his favor and guidance. Tell him what you are doing. Ask his advice. He knows more about fishing than Peter ever did. It would be such a pity that Peter should go home defeated when fish in abundance were within his reach—just the breadth of the boat away. Christ has provided the fish for the taking if you cast your net on the right side.

Handwritten Notes from God

And the scribes and Pharisees brought unto him a woman taken in adultery; and when they had set her in the midst, They say unto him, Master, this woman was taken in adultery, in the very act. Now Moses in the law commanded us, that such should be stoned: but what sayest thou? This they said, tempting him, that they might have to accuse him. But Jesus stooped down, and with his finger wrote on the ground, as though he heard them not... He that is without sin among you, let him first cast a stone at her. And again he stooped down, and wrote on the ground.

—John 8:3–8

A part of the earliest evidence of man's existence has been writings, etchings on the walls of caves, crude markings depicting scenes of the life events of that time. Pictures suggesting little more than scratches on cave walls depict beasts and human forms with weapons. These are man's efforts at records of communication. And of course, we are familiar with the advancement of this form of communication, which we call writing. Originally, these pictures and etchings were formulated in such a way as to tell a story. With that original concept in mind, letters or characters that serve as visible signs of ideas, words, or symbols are used to communicate or record a written composition.

You really didn't need to know all the historical details of writing to give you inspiration for your day; just know that God is in the communication business trying to establish and maintain a means or method of conveying his will to you. So God's first effort at written communication that we know of was brought to the people by Moses.

> And he gave unto Moses, when he had made an end of communing with him upon mount Sinai, two tables of testimony, tables of stone, written with the finger of God. And Moses turned, and went down from the mount, and the two tables of the testimony were in his hand: the tables were written on both their sides; on the one side and on the other were they written. And the tables were the work of God, and the writing was the writing of God, graven upon the tables. (Exodus 31:18, 32:15–16)

The law of God written on stone—it was unchangeable, not to be forgotten. I note that whatever was written in the presence of the adulterous woman was written not on unforgiving stone forever but upon the dust of the earth, subject to the blowing winds of the day. If Jesus wrote about sins, they were soon blown away, gone with the wind. In verification of the act of cleansing from sin in the presence of Jesus, we have this elegant communication: "Though your sins be as scarlet, they shall be as white as snow; though they be red like crimson, they shall be as wool."

Paul told us that Christ has "forgiven you all trespasses; Blotting out the handwriting of ordinances that was against us, which was contrary to us, and took it out of the way, nailing it to his cross." And now, he said, "Ye are manifestly declared to be the epistle of Christ, written not with ink but with the Spirit of the living God; not in tables of stone, but in fleshy tables of the heart."

The best part of this lesson on God's handwriting is this: "Your names are written in heaven."

Don't Get Caught Sitting on Your Pride

Confidence in an unfaithful man in time of trouble is like a broken tooth, and a foot out of joint.

—Proverbs 25:19

A broken tooth and a foot out of joint. One would think the wise man went overboard in trying to bring two divergent illustrations together to describe misplaced confidence in an unfaithful person. After all, the key phrase seems to be "in time of trouble." When you're in trouble, it's not the time for pleadings at a pep rally: "Don't fail me now. Don't fail me now!"

And, for sure, when they're serving BBQ ribs and T-bone steak, you don't want to feel something go *pop*, followed by an explosion of pain in your mouth as you spit out that new $1,200 crown your dentist said was "better than the original." Yeah right! Just when the eatin' was gonna be good!

Of course, 5 km in on the 15 km Sheaves for Christ hike is not a good time to step on a rock and twist your ankle. Man alive! Can you imagine the agony of having to hobble 5k back to the starting point, or (perish the thought) you decide you can make it to the finish line. I mean, that's ten more kilometers, okay? Who'd ever thought that little ol' rock; I mean, it was only the size of a golf ball!

So when I sat down in that nice chair to put on my shoes to go to Men's Prayer Meeting yesterday, I never even thought about that weakened leg I noticed when we moved. I had even said, "Gloria, when we get settled in, I'm going to fix this leg. It's got a weakened leg connection." Anyway, I was all dressed and ready for prayer meeting as I tugged at the last shoe when there was this sinking feeling and a twisting motion. And I was sitting on the floor with a sharp pain in my back as the chair's arm stabbed me between the shoulder blades. The chair's leg was now lying beside my human leg, and I was sitting in my church clothes, minus any dignity and a lot of pain. And I thought, "Lord, I'm on my way to Prayer Meeting. Why this now?"

And then I remembered my statement of good intention. I will fix it when I get settled in. Well, I didn't get settled in, but I did get settled down...on the floor, needing someone to help me get up (and I was really hoping for some of Gloria's sympathy). Now please understand, she did ask me if I was okay, but I noticed she was looking at the damaged chair when asking about me. But for my wife, it's "no blood, no glory," no bones sticking out. "I'm glad you're okay." Okey dokey, just fine! Have you ever calculated how long it takes for shattered pride to heal? Well how long would it have taken to fix a chair leg?

"Confidence in an unfaithful man in time of trouble is like a chair with a broken leg; it'll let you down unceremoniously on your pride when you least expect it."

It Was Not a Dream!

Then the hordes of all the nations that fight against Ariel (Jerusalem), that attack her and her fortress and besiege her, will be as it is with a dream, with a vision in the night—as when a hungry person dreams of eating, but awakens hungry still; as when a thirsty person dreams of drinking, but awakens faint and thirsty still. So will it be with the hordes of all the nations that fight against Mount Zion.

—Isaiah 29:7–8 (CEV)

Briefly, God determined to humble Jerusalem, and He employed Sennacherib, king of Assyria, as the means of achieving His justice. "He makes the wrath of man to praise Him." What a revelation is this of His absolute command over the fiercest and freest workings of the most depraved and rebellious of His creation! While wicked men execute the divine purpose, they frustrate their own. Sennacherib worked out the divine result, but all his own plans were like the visions of the starving traveler on the oriental desert, who—hungry, thirsty, and exhausted—lay down and dreamed under the heat of a tropical sun. He dreamed that he was eating and drinking but awoke only to discover to his great distress that both his hunger and thirst were but increased. Hell works out God's plans and frustrates its own. Heaven works out God's plans and fulfills its own.

Think of the man of our text who lay down to sleep under the raging desire for food and water? He dreamed that he was eating and drinking. His imagination created the very things for which his

169

appetite was craving. His imagination was the servant of his strongest appetites. Isn't this exactly as it is with the sinner! The appetite for the base motivations will create its visions of sensual pleasure. The appetite for worldly wealth will create its visions of fortune. The appetite for power will create its visions of social influence and applause. The sinner's imagination is always the servant of his strongest appetites and always pictures him in the most attractive scenarios he most strongly desires. But it's all a dream!

It is an illusory vision. The food and water of his dream were a mirage in the visionary desert; they only vanished into the air as his eyes opened. All the ideas of happiness entertained by the sinner are mental illusions. There are many theories of happiness entertained by man that are as elusive as the wildest dream.

Every notion for happiness is just so much smoke in the air if it is not centered around the Lord Jesus Christ. He, that is preparing intentionally for happiness, is not happy, nor can he be. "He that seeketh his life shall lose it." In the KJV our text reads, "An hungry man dreameth, and, behold, he eateth; but he awaketh, and his soul is empty." Every moral sleeper must awake either here or hereafter. As the army of Sennacherib were dreaming of a conquest, which had no real existence, so are there also multitudes of persons now dreaming that they are accomplishing the great object of their existence; but they are no more doing so than if they lay wrapped in the slumbers of the night.

Many years ago, when my wife and I were evangelizing, a beautiful family invited us to eat Sunday dinner. But there was something special about it. They were the owners of a very nice restaurant and buffet. We were invited to come for their buffet dinner one hour before they opened. We were the only guests in the restaurant. Their favorite expression seemed to be, "Here, try some of this." Perhaps the most wonderful thing is, you have an invitation also. Jesus has a table spread where the saints of God are fed. He invites His chosen people, "*Come and dine!*"

Prize-Winners for Pitiful

The steps of a good man are ordered by the
LORD: and he delighteth in his way. Though he
fall, he shall not be utterly cast down: for the
LORD upholdeth him with his hand.

—Psalm 37:23–24

The Geneva Bible observes, "God prospers the faithful because they walk in his ways with an upright conscience." The late T. F. Tenney said, "If God says, 'Yes,' I rejoice. If God says, 'No,' I can pout. But when God says, 'Wait,' it drives me straight up the wall. I've been slow in learning my basic premise of life is to learn so I can impart this knowledge to others." He also has stated that God directs our steps *and* our stops!

There he is, sitting on my desk next to my computer. He is a neat little guy and very faithful and persistent. He's been where he is for nearly twelve years. He's all bent over with his head down, and his trunk is literally lying all stretched out on the floor. This little elephant, by anybody else's standards, would be the prizewinner for pitiful. But it just depends on your observation skills. His head may be hanging low but perhaps not in discouragement but in prayer; for he has a sign that says it all: "Lord, help me to remember that nothing is going to happen to me today that you and I can't handle."

Steps are the incremental motion that moves mankind from place to place. The average stride of a male is thirty inches, but when the human body is under strain of attempting to lift a heavy load or to exert maximum force against an object (such as hitting a home run), there is a natural tendency to spread one's feet farther apart for more strength and better balance. God knows about lifting and moving heavy large objects as well as us. Listen: "Thou hast enlarged my steps under me; so that my feet did not slip" (2 Samuel 2:37).

Asaph wrote twelve psalms. Look at Psalm 73.

> No one can deny it—God is really good to Israel and to all those with pure hearts. But I nearly missed seeing it for myself. Here's my story: I narrowly missed losing it all. I was stumbling over what I saw with the wicked. For when I saw the boasters with such wealth and prosperity, I became jealous over their smug security. When I tried to understand it all, I just couldn't. It was too puzzling—too much of a riddle to me. But then one day I was brought into the sanctuaries of God, and in the light of glory, my distorted perspective vanished. Then I understood that the destiny of the wicked was near! (Psalm 73:1–17 TPT)

So to all you little elephants out there, don't be discouraged. Even if your trunk is lying on the ground, trust Jesus. He understands what you are going through. Be strong in the Lord and read Psalm 3:1–3 a few times. (It was written by David when he was running from his son Absalom.) "I have a lot of enemies, Lord. Many fight against me and say, 'God won't rescue you!' But thou, O Lord, art a shield for me; my glory, and the lifter up of mine head." The Contemporary English Version says, "And you give me victory and great honor" (Psalm 3:1–3). And thank you, Lord, for helping us when our trunk is on the ground.

The Four Way Cross

The God of our fathers raised up Jesus, whom ye slew and hanged on a tree.

—Acts 5:30

And we are witnesses of all things which he did both in the land of the Jews, and in Jerusalem; whom they slew and hanged on a tree.

—Acts 10:39

And when they had fulfilled all that was written of him, they took him down from the tree, and laid him in a sepulchre. But God raised him from the dead.

—Acts 13:29–30

Christ hath redeemed us from the curse of the law, being made a curse for us: for it is written, Cursed is every one that hangeth on a tree.

—Galatians 3:13

For even hereunto were ye called: because Christ also suffered for us, leaving us an example, that ye should follow his steps: Who his own self bare our sins in his own body on the tree, that we,

being dead to sins, should live unto righteousness: by whose stripes ye were healed.

—1 Peter 2:21, 24

Our neighbor's Ginkgo tree overhanging our backyard is approximately fifty-foot tall. Its branches are straight without curves or bends, covered with leaves shaped as fans, giving it somewhat of an oriental appearance. Primarily, the branches are visually pleasant, projecting upwards at a 45° angle. At the very top, the central branch can be seen growing straight up, approximately three feet farther than its closest branches. It is these branches that have my interest and attention. They do not grow at the 45° angle as do all the others. There are four of these branches protruding at a perfect 90° angle outward from the central branch (or trunk, if you will), parallel to the ground. Even more significantly, these four branches have grown to the four points of the compass: North, South, East, and West. They are distributed equidistant around the trunk (i.e., 90° apart). Thus, from every point of view, a cross can be seen. Because of the positioning of those four topmost branches, I refer to this phenome-non as The Four-Way Cross.

Beyond the unique beauty of this tree are at least three very interesting characteristics worthy of our attention today. Consider first the central branch: the trunk of the tree. It supports the entire structure of the tree in a beautifully balanced presentation. Pointing skyward, it would seem to remind us that the cross is the way to heaven. (1) Jesus is the way—there is no other. As one's eyes move upward along the trunk line of the tree, it is impossible to visually reach the top without passing the cross. Significantly, one cannot expect to see heaven without an encounter with the cross of Jesus Christ. Jesus said, "I am the way, the truth, and the life: no man cometh unto the Father, but by me" (John 14:6).

Perhaps, the most striking is the outreach of the four points of the cross. Neither Jew nor Greek, male nor female, rich nor poor are advantaged beyond another. (2) The cross reaches out to all—to black and white, from every tribe and nation and ethnic group to whosoever will. Because the cross points the way to Christ from the four points of the compass, all are bidden to come to Jesus from the North, South, East, and West.

Consider also the abbreviation for these compass points: NSEW. But if they are rearranged a bit, they could spell NEWS! The world today is experiencing a flood of bad news, the likes of which Noah encountered. (3) People desperately need some good news. And of course, the greatest news for people of all nations is the gospel of Jesus Christ, and it came by way of the cross.

Enough Is Enough!

And after [Ehud] was Shamgar the son of Anath,
which slew of the Philistines six hundred men
with an ox goad: and he also delivered Israel.

—Judges 3:31

In the days of Jael, the highways were unoccupied, and the travellers walked through byways. The inhabitants of the villages ceased; they ceased in Israel, until that I Deborah arose, that I arose a mother in Israel" (Judges 5:6–7). Oh my! This statement could occupy more than one page by itself! Suffice to say that God wants to put a boldness of the Holy Spirit within the mothers of the church, a boldness to get up and fight against the enemy for the souls of your children!

In the days of Shamgar and Jael, it seems that Deborah wanted to assure that we could identify the environment of Israel in this time of calamity. These are words descriptive of a state of weakness and fear, so much so that Israel could not openly use the highways but walked on hidden paths to avoid being seen by their enemies. It is a graphic description of a country occupied by an enemy. These Philistines had been running roughshod through the land, bullying God's people, and Shamgar wasn't taking anymore. Maybe like we do, he had been waiting for God to do something about it. But God was waiting for him because all He needs is someone He can use.

Deborah and Barak gave themselves to the will and purpose of God, and God wrought a mighty victory that day. Sisera, with his nine hundred chariots of iron and the entire army of the Canaanites, was defeated. "And the LORD discomfited Sisera, and all his chariots, and all his host, with the edge of the sword before Barak; so that Sisera lighted down off his chariot, and fled away on his feet. But Barak pursued after the chariots. And all the host of Sisera fell upon the edge of the sword; and there was not a man left. Howbeit Sisera fled away on his feet to the tent of Jael the wife of Heber the Kenite" (Judges 4:15–17). Jael had already lent herself to God for the purpose of bringing justice and vengeance to the Canaanites. The enemy was on the run. And when she saw Sisera escaping, she invited him into her tent for refreshment and rest, only to drive a tent peg through his skull while he slept."

Shamgar discovered he had rights. Jael discovered she had rights. She found out she could be a weapon of war for God. They were God's people. They had rights!—the right to own, the right to defend, the right to win, the right to live without fear. Do you know your rights today? Listen: "Keep the charge of the LORD thy God, to walk in his ways, to keep his statutes that thou mayest prosper in all that thou doest" (1 Kings 2:3). You have the right to succeed!

You also have the right to defend what God has given you. Don't surrender your family to the world. Remember, God keeps His promises. "All thy children shall be taught of the LORD; and great shall be the peace of thy children" (Isaiah 54:13). Shamgar wasn't talented; he was simply determined! And God honored that determination. He not only slew six hundred Philistines, but he also delivered an entire nation.

Today, it's time to tell the enemy of your soul, "Enough is enough!" Do your best, and let God do the rest!

Faint with Hunger but still Pursuing

And there came an angel of the LORD and sat under an oak, which was in Ophrah, that pertained unto Joash the Abiezrite: and his son Gideon threshed wheat by the winepress, to hide it from the Midianites. And the angel of the LORD appeared unto him, and said unto him, The LORD is with thee, thou mighty man of valor. And Gideon said unto him, Oh my Lord, if the LORD be with us, why then is all this befallen us? [Just because you are surrounded by the enemy does not indicate the absence of God!] and where be all his miracles which our fathers told us of, saying, Did not the LORD bring us up from Egypt? but now the LORD hath forsaken us, and delivered us into the hands of the Midianites. [Do not give God a bad rap based on what you assume to be the cause of your problems. He has a higher and greater purpose in mind for you...complete victory over your enemies!] And the LORD looked upon him, and said, Go in this (your personal encounter with God) thy might, and thou shalt save Israel from the hand of the Midianites: have not I sent thee?

—Judges 6:11–14

Those whom He calls, He also equips and empowers.

And when the primary battle was ending, when the Midianites were fleeing helter-skelter under the pursuit of Gideon and his three hundred men. "Gideon came to Jordan, and passed over, he, and the three hundred men that were with him, faint, yet pursuing them" (Judges 8:4). When they had crossed Jordan, Gideon asked for food from the men of Succoth of the tribe of Gad but was rebuffed and treated rudely. These were Israelites! But he moved on to the village of Penuel where he made the same request for food for his men, only to receive the same ill treatment. What was going on?

Gideon kept his priorities straight. The Midianite army troops were still out there to be conquered; only about fifteen thousand soldiers were left of all the troops of the Midianites: "for there fell a hundred and twenty thousand men that drew sword." Never mind the hunger; forget feeling faint. The Bible does not tell how or if Gideon and his men found food. Suffice it to say as Jesus once said to his disciples, "I have meat to eat that ye know not of." Gideon needed to finish what God had called him to do. He would deal with the problems of Succoth and Penuel later. First things first.

And Gideon smote the troops of the Midianites. "And when Zebah and Zalmunna fled, he pursued after them, and took the two kings of Midian, Zebah and Zalmunna, and discomfited all the host" (Judges 8:10–12). It is always so with the people of God. We sometimes encounter difficulties within the environment of the church. But we must not forget that the folks on the pew are not our enemies. They are our brothers and sisters! Our enemy is out there in the world. As for those on the pew, "the Lord knoweth them that are his" (2 Timothy 2:19).

The Case of the Runaway Choppers

Praise ye the LORD. Blessed is the man that feareth the LORD, that delighteth greatly in his commandments. His seed shall be mighty upon earth: the generation of the upright shall be blessed. Wealth and riches shall be in his house: and his righteousness endureth for ever. Unto the upright there ariseth light in the darkness: he is gracious, and full of compassion, and righteous. A good man sheweth favour, and lendeth: he will guide his affairs with discretion. Surely he shall not be moved forever: the righteous shall be in ever-lasting remembrance. He shall not be afraid of evil tidings: his heart is fixed, trusting in the LORD. His heart is established, he shall not be afraid, until he see his desire upon his enemies. He hath dispersed, he hath given to the poor; his righteousness endureth for ever; his horn shall be exalted with honour.

—Psalm 112:1–9

My heart is fixed, O God, my heart is fixed: I will sing and give praise.

—Psalm 57:7

> For God hath not given us the spirit of fear; but
> of power, and of love, and of a sound mind.
>
> —2 Timothy 1:7

Securely placed or fastened is the simple definition of *fixed*. Also, if something is fixed, we usually assume it has been repaired. Or if an athletic event, election, or some sort of contest has been fixed, we understand that someone arranged for the outcome ahead of the event, giving rise to the saying, "the fix is in."

There used to be a product for cementing dentures in one's mouth called Fixodent. With no intent to embarrass, this gummy goo did not always work. It could (and often did) let go right in the middle if one's speaking, much to the embarrassment of the denture wearer and the often-hilarious entertainment of the audience. A true story was told of one of our beloved elders who was preaching a Revival service with great exuberance when the unfortunate happened. His dentures came flying out of his mouth, sailed over the top of the pulpit to the floor, rolling in amongst the congregation. "Everybody, lift your hands and worship the Lord" was his immediate loose-lipped cry. Hastening down into the altar area, he spotted his runaway choppers right between the feet of a dear Sister. Stretching his hand forth to retrieve the "gates of pearl," his hand accidentally brushed the leg of the dear worshiping Sister. She gasped as her eyes flew open, and she saw the preacher, exclaiming, "Oh! Brother So-and-So!" To which he replied, "Keep your mind on God, Sister. Keep your mind on God!" Humorous and true, one can be sure, he wanted the people's mind to be fixed on God better than his dentures had been fixed in his mouth.

There are so many diversions and distractions, which challenge the saint of God. We must possess a rock-solid determination to stay focused on God, on the moving of His Spirit amongst us. Jeremiah tells us that God knows "the thoughts that I think toward you, saith the LORD, thoughts of peace, and not of evil, to give you an expected end" (Jeremiah 29:11). This being so, His plans can be aborted by distractions if we do not stay focused on the Spirit. Paul reminded us in Romans 8 "that they that are after the Spirit [do mind] the things of the Spirit."

I earnestly urge us all to live with a made-up mind. The Psalmist said, "My heart is fixed." By the way, if something is fixed, we usually assume it has been repaired. Because God gives us a sound mind.

Reverend Damien

The late Ravi Zacharias told the story of a man named Damien whose brother died while working with a group of leprosy victims on the island of Molokai, Hawaii. It was while Damien was visiting his brother that he unexpectedly died, leaving the leprosy victims without anyone to help them or give them aide.

Seeing their awful plight, Damien plunged right into the work that his brother had started and took over where he left off. He was so deeply affected by the terrible disease and suffering of these poor people that soon he found he was unable to ignore them. He must do what he could to help them.

The Hawaiian government was sending more and more of the leprous people to the colony on Molokai. Damien gave his very best efforts to care for them, even though the risk of him getting leprosy was so likely. "Do not touch them!" he was warned over and over, but he felt their pain and suffering so much that he assisted them any way he could, which often involved lifting, washing, changing bandages.

One day, as he was fixing himself a cup of tea, he accidentally spilled a cup of boiling water on his foot. In a moment, he realized he did not feel any pain. Carefully, he poured a bit of hot water on his other foot and, feeling no pain. knew without doubt that he was now leprous.

When they gathered for their Sunday morning worship. his customary greeting was, "My fellow believers…" That morning, he began the time of worship with his greeting but with somewhat of a change. It was, "My fellow lepers…!"

Reverend Damien was from the country of Belgium. When he eventually died of his leprous disease, he was buried in the cemetery there on the island of Molokai. However, after a bit of time, the

Belgian government decided they should repatriate the body to the land of his birth. So they prepared to exhume his body to take him home to Belgium.

Hearing of these plans, the leaders of the leper colony protested, saying, "Reverend Damien served us here. Indeed he gave his life for us here. Could you at least cut off his right arm and hand and leave them buried here in his grave? It was his hands that touched our lives. Leave his hand here."

And they did. In a cemetery on the island of Molokai is a tombstone bearing the name of Reverend Damien, missionary to the lepers of Hawaii. However, the grave only contains the arm and hand of a man who so loved them that he gave even his life to them.

Mahalia Jackson would sing: "If I can help somebody as I pass along, If I can cheer somebody with a word or song. If I can show somebody, that he's traveling wrong, Then my living shall not be in vain."

When God Says, "Let's Go for A Walk."

But now thus saith the LORD that created thee, O Jacob, and he that formed thee, O Israel, Fear not: for I have redeemed thee, I have called thee by thy name; thou art mine. When thou passest through the waters, I will be with thee; and through the rivers, they shall not overflow thee: when thou walkest through the fire, thou shalt not be burned; neither shall the flame kindle upon thee. For I am the LORD thy God, the Holy One of Israel, thy Saviour:

—Isaiah 43:1–3

O the depth of the riches both of the wisdom and knowledge of God! how unsearchable are his judgments, and his ways past finding out! For who hath known the mind of the Lord? or who hath been his counsellor? Or who hath first given to him, and it shall be recompensed unto him again? For of him, and through him, and to him, are all things: to whom be glory forever. Amen.

—Romans 11:33–36

I find it rather remarkable that God loves to take walks with His created image, mankind. For instance, Enoch walked with God. And in Genesis 5, we are told that Enoch was 65 years old when his son Methuselah was born; and Enoch walked with God for 300 years after Methuselah was born and continued to raise his family of sons and daughters. And Enoch lived to be 365 years old, and he still walked with God (are you ready for this?), and he was not; for God took him." *He did not die...ever!*

Someone with a lively imagination (which I happen to appreciate) said, "God and Enoch were walking together one day, as they often did, and they walked farther than anticipated. God said to Enoch, 'Enoch, you and I have been walking together for such a long while. We are much nearer my home than yours. Come on home with me for now, and you can rest and refresh yourself!' So, Enoch simply went home with the Lord."

Enoch's son Methuselah—now that man just kept on living for 969 years! His son Lamech had a son, named Noah, whom they believed would somehow help them survive in their world, which was growing increasingly more wicked. With passage of time, Noah was 500 years old; and there were three sons in his family: Shem, Ham, and Japheth. These were the generations of Noah whom the Bible declares to have been just men and perfect in their generations. Oh, and Noah walked with God.

And when Abram was 99 years old, the LORD appeared to him and said, "I am the Almighty God. Walk before me, and be thou perfect." Our Father might say, "Son, I want you to come for a walk with me. So stay beside me and behave yourself!" This "be thou perfect" business sometimes causes a lot of frustration and problems for children of God. "Can't nobody be perfect!" they say. "The only perfect person was hung on a cross," they say. "What if He takes me through the fire?" they say. Well, *through* means you made it out!

But the Bible says, "Christ glorified not himself to be made a high priest; but he that said unto him, Thou art my Son, today have I begotten thee. Who in the days of his flesh, when he had offered up prayers and supplications with strong crying and tears unto him that was able to save him from death, and was heard in that he feared; Though he were a Son, yet learned he obedience by the things which he suffered; And being made perfect, he became the author of eternal salvation unto all them that obey him" (Hebrews 5:5–10).

If You Want to Feel Rich...

There is that scattereth, and yet increaseth; and there is that withholdeth more than is meet, but it tendeth to poverty.

—Proverbs 11:24

There is that maketh himself rich, yet hath nothing: there is that maketh himself poor, yet hath great riches.

—Proverbs 13:7

If you don't mind, I thought it might benefit to talk a bit about how you handle your purse or wallet. For years, when hearing preachers talk about people's spending habits, I've heard such statements as, "If you want to know about a person's relationship with God, look at their spending habits." So here's a little food for thought regarding *man* and his money. I will give quotation credit where I can if I can. Here goes.

What God orders, He pays for. And for sure, where God guides, He provides. *O. S. Hawkins* is quoted as saying, "The principal hindrance to the advancement of the kingdom of God is greed. It is the chief obstacle to heaven-sent revival. It seems that when the back of greed is broken, the human spirit soars into regions of unselfishness. I believe that it is safe to say there can be no continuous revival without cheerful (hilarious) giving. And I fear no contradiction: wherever there is 'hilarious' giving there will soon be revival!"

A Christian can never serve God *and* money, but they must learn to serve God *with* money. I hope you're not too uncomfortable with this subject, for our intention is to help us all to look at our financial habits. *Brian Kluth* said, "Money talks. It says 'goodbye.' If you doubt this, answer the question: How much money did I make in the last ten years? Then answer, How much do I have left? Also ask, 'And how much do I have stored in heaven?'"

Have you considered that the most expensive vehicle to operate, per mile, is the shopping cart? Credit is what keeps you from knowing how far past broke you are. Consider the number of years it takes to pay off an $8,000 credit card balance at 18 percent with minimal monthly payments. Brace yourself, it is fifty-four years!

> I never would have been able to tithe the first million dollars I ever made if I had not tithed my first salary, which was $1.50 per week. (John D. Rockefeller Sr. [1839–1937], American industrialist and philanthropist)

> God's work done in God's way will never lack God's supply. (J. Hudson Taylor [1832–1905], English missionary to China)

If you want to feel rich, just count all the things you have that money can't buy. I'd recommend that you do your giving while you're living so you'll be knowing where it's going.

Now a final thought: When you give to God, you discover that God gives to you. And so He does. Amen.

I Remember When...

Remember the days of old, consider the years of many generations: ask thy father, and he will shew thee; thy elders, and they will tell thee.

—Deuteronomy 32:7

We Will Remember
by Tommy Walker

We will remember, we will remember
We will remember the works of Your hands
We will stop and give you praise
For great is Thy faithfulness

You're our creator, our life sustainer
Deliverer, our comfort, our joy
Throughout the ages You've been our shelter
Our peace in the midst of the storm

With signs and wonders You've shown Your power
With precious blood You showed us Your grace
You've been our helper, our liberator
The giver of life with no end

We will remember, we will remember
We will remember the works of Your hands
We will stop and give you praise
For great is Thy faithfulness

When we walk through life's darkest valleys
We will look back at all You have done
And we will shout, our God is good
And He is the faithful One

I still remember the day You saved me
The day I heard You call out my name
You said You loved me and would never leave me
And I've never been the same

This wonderful and powerful worship song does exactly that; it elicits memories from times past of the works of His hands, memories of His help, how He liberated us; it even elicits memories of His presence that was there when we walked through life's darkest valleys. Most of all, I still remember the day He saved me, the day I heard Him call out my name. He said He loved me and would never leave me, and I've never been the same.

Shortly after "entering into the ministry" (I was just a day past my nineteenth birthday), Mike and I were "practicing" our preaching skills in my home. We were attempting to hone our public speaking ability by preaching and quoting scriptures to each other. He would take five minutes, then I would speak for five minutes, using my wife's ironing board for a pulpit, which we had strategically placed in the living room near the kitchen. (I did mention strategically, right?) Gloria could listen to the preachers tossing in an encouraging "Amen," or "Hallelujah" while she was preparing *pizza* for the after-church snack—very strategic.

Well, long story short, Gloria, in turning on the propane oven, did not realize it had not lighted properly. As Mike was bringing his five minute "Revival Sermon" to a "fill-up-the-altar" conclusion, suddenly there was a terrific explosion! My three-month-pregnant wife went sailing through the air, folded in half like a hairpin, landing in a heap under the kitchen table. The windows in the kitchen and living room were blown out. Mike thought it happened because of his preaching. I had immediately run to my wife, but he thought I was "going up in the rapture." He wouldn't take his eyes off me, lest

I began to ascend into the heavens. When we all were able to determine that, miraculously, there were no injuries to anyone, especially the *pizza* cook, we sat around discussing the explosive events of the evening.

"Mike," my wife said, "why were you looking so intently at my husband?"

"Oh," he said, "I wanted to make sure that if he went up, I was too."

Folks, "all is well that ends well," they say. One day it *will* happen, "for the Lord himself shall descend from heaven with a shout, with the voice of the archangel, and with the trump of God: and the dead in Christ shall rise first: Then we which are alive and remain shall be caught up together with them in the clouds, to meet the Lord in the air: and so shall we ever be with the Lord."

A Note of WARNING!

When the people come to worship the LORD at
any festival, those who enter by the north gate
are to leave by the south gate after they have wor-
shiped, and those who enter by the south gate are
to leave by the north gate. No one may go out by
the same way he entered, but must leave by the
opposite gate.

—Ezekiel 46:9

David Ingles penned words for a song that are so appropriate to
this scripture text:

I won't go home the way I came, in Jesus Name. I won't be
bound, oppressed, tormented, sick, or lame; for the Holy Ghost of
Acts is still the same. I won't go home the way I came in Jesus Name.

Solemn feasts are times of worship and seeking after God. These
are life-changing experiences. The Lord wanted not only His people,
Israel, to know this; but indeed, He wanted all worshippers through
the ages to know the dynamic power of worship. To achieve this, He
sent the prophet Jeremiah to the Potter's House for an object lesson.

The word which came to Jeremiah from the
LORD, saying, Arise, and go down to the potter's
house, and there I will cause thee to hear my
words. Then I went down to the potter's house,
and, behold, he wrought a work on the wheels.
And the vessel that he made of clay was marred
in the hand of the potter: so he made it again

another vessel, as seemed good to the potter to
make it. (Jeremiah 18:1–4)

The vessel was marred in the Potter's hand; but because this
happened, the potter made it again, and it was changed...for good.
It's good to be in the church when tragedy happens! Jeremiah's experience at the Potter's house left him changed. It was a visible change. It
also was a physical change. But most of all, it was a spiritual change.
I sometimes believe that those who enter the house of God should be
given a disclaimer with the following words of warning:

Warning!

Claiming fellowship with Jesus and his disciples will change
your life. Those who totally give themselves over to following
Christ will be remarkably and dramatically changed. You can
expect friends and family to notice an alteration in lifestyle, dress,
speech, and habits.

You should be aware that certain side effects will accompany
association with Jesus Christ and His people. Don't be alarmed;
these issues are not life-threatening but life altering. Believers find
that their life is extended beyond this life only and that there is
a valid expectation of eternal life! Some of the side effects to be
expected are unexplainable tendencies to burst out in joyful singing, tendencies to pray and to read the Bible, cravings to attend
the House of God known as Church. Some have been known
to burst out speaking in an unknown language; others lift their
hands and shout, "Hallelujah." I would leave a note of *warning*!
Anyone thinking of becoming a Christian should give serious
consideration to the proven fact that, once it happens, you will
never be the same again!

The Bush Is on Fire; Take a Look!

One day while Moses was taking care of the sheep and goats of his father-in-law Jethro, [who was] the priest of Midian, he led the flock across the desert and came to Sinai, the holy mountain. There the angel of the LORD appeared to him as a flame coming from the middle of a bush. Moses saw that the bush was on fire but that it was not burning up. "This is strange," he thought. "Why isn't the bush burning up? I will go closer and see." When the LORD saw that Moses was coming closer, he called to him from the middle of the bush and said, "Moses! Moses!" He answered, "Yes, here I am." God said, "Do not come any closer. Take off your sandals, because you are standing on holy ground."

—Exodus 3:1–5 (GNB)

Moses was employed as a shepherd when he was honored with this divine visitation. God encourages us to work. God is well pleased when he finds us employed. Moses was alone on the desert with his sheep. Solitude is a good friend to be used for our communion with God. When we are alone, the Father is with us. Moses saw more of God in a desert than he had ever seen in Pharaoh's court.

In the case of Moses and the burning bush, we should do well to take the Bible at its word, neither denying nor fabricating what is being said. Your KJV Bible, and mine, gives us a very clear and distinctive picture of the event. Look at it closely: "And the angel of the LORD appeared unto him in a flame of fire out of the midst of a bush: and he looked, and, behold, the bush burned with fire, and the bush was not consumed. And Moses said, I will now turn aside, and see this great sight, why the bush is not burnt" (Exodus 3:2–3 KJV). There was no external force nor substance nor action mentioned or suggested as causing the bush to burn. It just did!

My friends, when God wants to use you or speak to you, He doesn't need anyone or anything to light your fire; not loud music, flashing lights, nor charismatic preachers blowing on you, pushing you, or barking like a dog(?). God doesn't require silly gimmicks and blatant tom-foolery to ignite a flame of desire for revival. He will supply both the flame and the heat if you will provide the wood.

The use of gimmicks will diminish the voice of God that would speak to us out of the bush. But if we can see the flame, and if we can see the bush not consumed, and if we will turn aside from our own pursuits, then, and only then, will instruction and revelation come to us—instruction that makes us know that the "sandals of our life" must come off, for we are standing on holy ground. Then comes the revelation of who God is. "I *am* the God of thy father, the God of Abraham, the God of Isaac, and the God of Jacob. And Moses hid his face; for he was afraid to look upon God" (Exodus 3:6). Bare your feet but hide your face. Our feet take us wherever we desire to go. That is seen by God. He knows our pursuits, where we've been, or where we're going! Cover your face in humility and worship. Perhaps not literally but behind the covered face, we can search our hearts as we stand before the mighty God. Consider this one with whom we have to do, for He is the God who never changes!

The Bottom Line

I can do all things through Christ which strengtheneth me.

—Philippians 4:13 (KJV)

Whatever I have, wherever I am, I can make it through anything in the One who makes me who I am.

—Philippians 4:13 (MSG)

I have the strength to face all conditions by the power that Christ gives me.

—Philippians 4:13 (GNB)

Finally, my brethren, be strong in the Lord, and in the power of his might. Praying always with all prayer and supplication in the Spirit, and watching thereunto with all perseverance and supplication for all saints.

—Ephesians 6:10, 18

The story comes of Roger Reynolds. In 1974, he was with the world renown Golden Knights parachute team of Charlottesville, Virginia. He was on his 959th jump. He had two parachutes, one main and one emergency. At 2,800 feet, chute #1 failed; 202 feet later, chute #2 failed. He landed in a doctor's front yard with a terrible thud and no chute. He was knocked unconscious. The doctor happened to be there and rushed out to help. Roger's leg swelled like a watermelon. His foot was pointing backward. His anklebone was sticking out. His left heel was smashed. In addition to this, he had an open compound fracture on the shinbone. He had torn cartilages in his knees. His hip was cracked. His pelvis was cracked. His tailbone was broken. He had three broken ribs, a broken wrist, a broken forearm, a broken upper arm, a dislocated shoulder, and concussions.

Roger was flat on his back for five months. He fainted the first time they sat him in a wheelchair. He fainted the first time on the parallel bars. But he kept sneaking into the gym to train even when they told him not to. In August 1975, Roger was released from the hospital. He jumped again. He trained for two years and, in 1978, ran and finished the twenty-six-mile Boston Marathon. He refused to give up. That's the bottom line.

The definition of perseverance is the continued effort to do or achieve something despite difficulties, failure, or opposition—the Bible calls it steadfastness—when faced with a difficult task and all within you is screaming, "Just quit!"

When your weary body is telling you it's much easier to throw in the towel that if you do, the pain will end. And the phrase repeats itself: "End the pain! End the pain!" But from the recesses of your kindergarten class come the echo of *The Little Engine Who Thought He Could.* And regardless of how steep the mountain is that's confronting you, the childhood memory begins to rhythmically chant with the cadence of a little steam engine: "I think I can. I think I can." Then as the summit is in view, the tone changes: "I know I can! I know I can!" And one more time, a change is heard. "I knew I could! I knew I could! And the victory is precious as the little engine continues on its way, persevering steadfastly."

> Therefore, my beloved brethren, be ye stedfast, unmoveable, always abounding in the work of the Lord, forasmuch as ye know that your labour is not in vain in the Lord. (1 Corinthians 15:58)

The Fight

Fight the good fight of faith, lay hold on eternal life, whereunto thou art also called, and hast professed a good profession before many witnesses.

—1 Timothy 6:12

The late Muhammad Ali recalled a fight against Sonny Liston for the heavyweight title in January 1964. "Liston was the strongest man I'd ever fought," said Ali. "Every time I hit him, it hurt me worse than it did him. I gave him everything I had. When the sixth round ended, I was completely spent. I couldn't even raise my arms. I couldn't even stand up to go back into the ring. 'I'm goin' home!' I told my trainer Angelo Dundee. 'I'm not goin' back in there.'" Hearing this, Dundee demanded that Ali get ready to go in. But the fighter refused. The bell rang, and still Ali didn't rise. Dundee pushed him and shouted, "Get in there, and don't come out until you are the heavyweight champion of the world." Ali struggled to his feet. Liston didn't. Muhammad Ali won the title by just getting back up one more time than his opponent.

Rarely are fights totally one-sided. Hardly ever does a fighter win without taking at least a few blows. We are in warfare against wandering stars, fallen angels, and rebel spirits who are manifesting the same insurrection as Lucifer in his original rebellion. You may feel like Ali, like you've given everything you have. You've given your blood, sweat, and tears for the work of the Lord and the ministry to his people. You may feel like giving up and that "bearing the burdens of others" is too painful because you haven't seen the results that you were hoping for.

Remember: You may be wounded, but you're not slain! You may have lost this "round," but you haven't lost the fight! You may have lost this battle, but you haven't lost the war! There are "forces" that will tell you, "Don't try again. Don't risk your heart. Don't bear the burdens of others because in the past, it has left you bloodied, bruised, and broken into more pieces than shattered crystal." But with the "ears of the Spirit," you hear the cry of the Spirit calling out to you! This cry is pushing, propelling, and persuading you. It's the Spirit of God. It's the plan and purpose of God in your life, calling out to you to get back up and get back into the good fight of faith. The Lord has seen your efforts for Him and will heal and restore you to "fighting strength." He has seen your tears and prayers of intercession. Your tears and prayers are never wasted.

> I have heard thy prayer, I have seen thy tears:
> behold, I will heal thee. (2 Kings 20:5)

Listen to the words from an old English ballad: "I will lay me down and bleed a while. Though I am wounded, I am not slain; I shall rise and fight again." The whole host of heaven is in your "corner." Rise back up in prayer. Rise back up in intercession. Rise back up in fasting. Keep drawing in the hurting. Keep reaching out to the discouraged. Keep lifting up the weak. Keep pulling down the strongholds. And keep on fighting the good fight. This is no time to let up. This is no time to give up. This is no time to back up. But it is time to stand up and be counted as a Soldier of the Cross!

> Rejoice not against me, O mine enemy: when I
> fall, I shall arise; when I sit in darkness, the Lord
> shall be a light unto me. (Micah 7:8)

If you never surrender, one day, when this life is over, as you make your way toward the throne of God with slow and heavy step, you'll unbuckle and cast aside your dented shield. You'll pull off and drop your battle-scarred helmet. They will help pry your fingers from around the handle of the two-edged sword, and you'll lay it down for the last and final time. Then as you stand before His throne, you'll hear the Captain of your salvation say those priceless words, "Well done, thou good and faithful servant."

No Hiding Place

And it shall come to pass afterward, *that* I will pour out my spirit upon all flesh; and your sons and your daughters shall prophesy, your old men shall dream dreams, your young men shall see visions: And also, upon the servants and upon the handmaids in those days will I pour out my spirit. And I will shew wonders in the heavens and in the earth, blood, and fire, and pillars of smoke. The sun shall be turned into darkness, and the moon into blood, before the great and the terrible day of the LORD come. And it shall come to pass, *that* whosoever shall call on the name of the LORD shall be delivered.

—Joel 2:28–32

The immediate and urgent occasion for this book is a huge national calamity in the form of a great plague of locusts more terrible than anything of the kind that has happened within living memory. Let's go back to the prophet: "Hear this, ye old men, and give ear, all ye inhabitants of the land. Hath this been in your days, or even in the days of your fathers? Tell ye your children of it, and let your children tell their children, and their children another generation" (Joel 1:2–4). These locusts were like an invading army, darkening the sky, swift in their advancement, with a sound like crackling flames burning dry stubble. Climbing city walls, entering houses by the windows and doors, they devoured everything in their path. A land like the garden of *Eden* was left like a desolate barren wilderness.

Joel cried out for the calamity of sin sweeping across Israel, hence the description of the palmerworm, the locust, the cankerworm, and the caterpillar. Look at the description used by the NIV: "What the locust swarm has left the great locusts have eaten; what the great locusts have left the young locusts have eaten; what the young locusts have left other locusts have eaten" (Joel 1:4).

Never have we heard so much about E. coli (in the food), fecal chloroform contamination (in the water of our beaches), foot-and-mouth disease (in our cattle), AIDS and HIV infection, and now COVID-19.

One is reminded of the prophecy of Amos: "[It is] as if a man did flee from a lion, and a bear met him; or went into the house, and leaned his hand on the wall, and a serpent bit him" (Amos 5:19).

Bro. and Sis. Nathaniel Urshan used to sing this song. The crowd loved it. One of the verses said, "The devil wears a hypocrite shoe. The devil wears a hypocrite shoe. Oh, the devil wears a hypocrite shoe. Better watch out; he'll put it on you. Oh, there's no hiding place down here." The main stanza was very powerful: "There's no hiding place down here. There's no hiding place down here. Well I run to the rock just to hide my face. And the rocks cried out, no hiding place. There's no hiding place down here." We must not ever believe that we are sufficient in and of ourselves against the tribulations of these last days. Only the blood of Jesus can hide our sins from the Holy One on the throne, and that same blood will hide us from the onslaught of the enemy.

This is a very good time to call upon the Lord for deliverance. Call on Him now. Oh, Rock of Ages, hide Thou me.

Save the Scraps

If a man deliver unto his neighbour an ass, or an ox, or a sheep, or any beast, to keep; and it die, or be hurt, or driven away, no man seeing it: Then shall an oath of the LORD be between them both, that he hath not put his hand unto his neighbour's goods; and the owner of it shall accept thereof, and he shall not make it good. And if it be stolen from him, he shall make restitution unto the owner thereof. If it be torn in pieces, then let him bring it for witness, and he shall not make good that which was torn.

—Exodus 22:10–13

Thus saith the LORD; As the shepherd taketh out of the mouth of the lion two legs, or a piece of an ear; so shall the children of Israel be taken out [of the mouth of their enemies] that dwell in Samaria.

—Amos 3:12

That which was torn of beasts I brought not unto thee; I bare the loss of it.

—Genesis 31:39

Jacob makes a strong argument to Laban regarding his integrity of accountability for his role as a shepherd under his father-in-law, Laban. Both Jacob and Laban knew that sheep sometimes fall prey to wolves and lions.

So Jacob presented his case based on the ways of wild beasts. He knew, as an under shepherd, what the lion had left. He must show to his master proof that he was not stealing sheep for his own use or for some private sale for gain. To produce the scraps of a slain sheep usually meant that the lion had to be challenged in the act of devouring his prey. It is the most daring thing, and not usual, for a shepherd to take anything out of a lion's mouth, though David did. And we are not talking about the rescue of a whole sheep or lamb, but bits and pieces, the scraps as it were. There is little left for recognition when a lion has been chewing on its prey, especially when the lion has satisfied his hunger with the best of it, perhaps two shanks of the legs that had no flesh upon them and the gristle of the ear (so says the Targum). The point being made that only a few of the Israelites (and in our case, our loved ones) should escape the enemy.

Jeremiah offers a prophetical view of this matter, saying, "Israel is a scattered sheep; the lions have driven him away [from worshiping the true God, Jehovah]: first the king of Assyria hath devoured him; and last this Nebuchadrezzar king of Babylon hath broken his bones" (Jeremiah 50:17). Always, the law of the wild is that what the lion doesn't devour, the jackals will and the foxes and the vultures!

Cristy Lane's lyrics encourage us to "Wrap up all the shattered dreams of your life, and at the feet of Jesus lay them down." She writes, "Give them all. Give them all to Jesus. Shattered dreams—wounded hearts, broken toys. And He will turn your sorrows into joy." Christy also gave us a solid dose of reality: "He never said you'd only see sunshine. He never said there'd be no rain. He only promised us a heart full of singing. That's the very thing that once brought you pain." Friends, nothing is harder to deal with than having to see the scraps of potential and promise, beauty and blessing, and hearing the words echo off the walls of your broken heart, "It might have been..."

I offer you this hope based in the truth that it is "'not by might nor yet by power but by my Spirit,' saith the Lord of hosts." You see, the scraps were once a living, breathing creature. So I ask, "Have you ever heard of the Valley of Dry Bones? Does that God still live today?" What he's done for others, He'll do for you!

The Fellowship of Believers

And when the day of Pentecost was fully come, they were all with one accord in one place. And all that believed were together...

—Acts 2:1, 42

In the animal world of nature, there are many various names for fellowship: There is a gaggle of geese, a murder of crows (I'm serious), a flock of chickens, a pod of whales, a ball of snakes, a school of fish, a covey of quails, a pride of lions, a herd of cattle, and—surprise, surprise—a crowd of people. So, in the language of our text, "And when the day of Pentecost was fully come, they were all with one accord in one place. And all that believed were together." They were not just a crowd, they were the *church*!

"Two are better than one," and "if one prevail against him, two shall withstand him; and a threefold cord is not quickly broken" (Ecclesiastes 4:9, 12). And also, "Where no counsel is, the people fall: but in the multitude of counsellors there is safety" (Proverbs 11:14). "For by wise counsel thou shalt make thy war: and in multitude of counsellors there is safety" (Proverbs 24:6). This Acts 2:38 experience of repentance, water baptism in Jesus Name, and the Holy Spirit baptism with speaking in other tongues was not done in a corner. It was proclaimed by the apostle Peter on the day of Pentecost and was experienced by, first, 120 people in an upper room, then eventually over three thousand people that day.

Friends, that was quite a crowd of people having fellowship. I believe that Satan is dancing around the world as he watches church after church closing because of an invisible sickness. That is not to say that the sickness isn't real. Indeed, it is. But Satan is dancing because the strength and effectiveness of God's people has been decimated by the inactivity of God's people, *the believers*! While we do not advocate disobedience to those in authority, no one is preventing the church from earnest prayer and fasting. We must put a stop to the lethargy and idleness of a self-induced quarantine of spiritual power.

We must awaken ourselves and accept the fact that the problems facing us are not going away on their own. We must seek the face of God for a mighty overthrow of the bondage that has brought most of us to a standstill spiritually. It is time for God's people to come together! We're not a crowd isolated from each other; we're the church! We are socially distanced. But now is the time to get together in desperation before the throne of God. Every chain must be broken, and every wall must come down!

Don't Let a Clown
Ruin Your Parade

Marching bands have always intrigued me. I always get goosebumps and even teary-eyed at parades when I stand on the street at curbside and watch the bands come marching along all in cadence, in step, trumpets blaring, the drum major high stepping so proudly. Oh yes! I've marched in bands myself, played my saxophone, and marched down Main Street in our annual hometown Christmas parade, playing "Here Comes Santa Claus."

It was hard work. Not only did we have to practice our music and get the song down pat, but we also had to go out to the football field and practice marching and marching and marching—left, right, left, right, all in step, get it right, left, right. And just when we got it, Mr. Engstrom said that we now had to learn how to turn left and turn right. Because parades don't always march straight down a street. Sometimes they turn corners, all in unison, staying in cadence now and turning like a swinging gate. Inside corner, take baby steps; outside corner, take giant steps; keep the ranks straight. Look sharp now. Left, right. We got it right.

Now you had a piece of cake if you played the flute or clarinet. They were very light, weighed almost nothing. But I felt sorry for the tuba guy, or, well, even I felt sorry for myself. That tenor saxophone was not a piece of cake. After marching eight or ten blocks with that hanging around your neck, you felt like asking Mr. Engstrom if maybe he needed another piccolo in the band and the drums.

We were invited to march in a parade in a neighboring town. Mr. Engstrom announced this news item during band practice one day. We got excited. Man, we must really be good. they wanted us to come march in their parade. At the end of practice, Mr. Engstrom called me aside.

"Mason, my drummer can't make it for this parade, so I need you to play the drum."

Uh-oh! He said, The Drum, as in the Big Bass Drum! Man, like, that thing was huge. So there I stood, twelve years old, a whopping 103-pound, skinny kid (I'm telling you guys the reality here.), waiting while Mr. Engstrom adjusted the straps on that gigantic machine.

"Who needs lessons, right!" He said, "You set the cadence—left, right, left, right. Hit the drum with this." He handed me a big fuzzy ball tied to the end of a stick.

Left (*Boom*), right (*Boom*), left (*Boom*), right (*Boom*).

"Man, you got it!" He said. "You're a natural."

I found out that band teachers would say anything when they needed someone to play The Big Bass Drum!

Parade Day—*boom, boom, boom, boom*. This wasn't too bad. Left, right.

"Hey, Kid! Let me have your drumstick. Quick." A clown (for real—big, round, red nose, goofy-looking hair, size 29 shoes going *flop, flop, flop*) wanted my drumstick, my cadence setter. What was I going to say? Go jump in the lake. There was no lake here, so I gave it to him. That crazy clown started beating My Bass Brum out of cadence. No left, right, left, right. More like Boomity, Boomity, Bop, Bop. He had our band so confused and out of step. It was chaos! Mr. Engstrom came running from somewhere up front, and I got my drumstick back—left, right, left, right in unison. We were a band, marching on to victory, keeping a lookout for clowns. They were not as funny as they look!

Oh, one day, there will be another Parade.

There'll be singing; there'll be shouting

When the saints come marching home. In Jerusalem, in Jerusalem, Waving palms with loud hosannas as the King shall take His throne. In the new Jerusalem.

Till the Storm Passes By

The last two days and nights had been exceptionally stormy. Very high winds with heavy rain seemed to be the main items on the weather menu. Our neighbor's large Frosty the Snowman (wire and plastic variety) blew over. Christmas deco littered the street around our house. The last hold-on leaves finally gave up amidst the huffing and puffing of the wind, leaving the trees bare and cold looking.

My beloved Biblically astute wife drew my attention to the fact that the Bible is known to declare on occasion (452 times): "it came to pass." She observed that regardless of how heavy the storm, it shall pass. We need not fret with all its howling. It will pass by sooner or later. Sometimes, the little child inside of us feels a bit frightened because of all the bluster. The storms of life do that, too.

Mosie Lister, songwriter, singer, and preacher, wrote a beautiful song concerning this very matter: the fear generated by storms—the natural kind as well as the internal kind experienced by humans. If you have opportunity, it will be well worth your time to listen to this great gospel classic.

Till the Storm Passes By

In the dark of the midnight have I oft hid my face,
While the storm howls above me, and there's no hiding place.
Mid the crash of the thunder, Precious Lord, hear my cry,
Keep me safe till the storm passes by.

Many times Satan whispered, "There is no need to try,
For there's no end of sorrow, there's no hope by and by."

But I know Thou art with me, and tomorrow I'll rise,
Where the storms never darken the skies.

Chorus
Till the storm passes over, till the thunder sounds no more,
Till the clouds roll forever from the sky;
Hold me fast, let me stand in the hollow of Thy hand,
Keep me safe till the storm passes by.

Let me pray for you. "Dear Lord, more than anyone of us can know, you are acquainted with storms. You have faced the storms of doubt and unbelief, storms of hatred and strife, storms of disease, of anger, of distrust. But, Jesus, you have proven the power of your spoken Word. Storms ceased, and winds stopped at your Word. And so, Lord, for my brothers and sisters and the beautiful young people and children, I ask of you for their sakes; do it again. Speak a word into their lives, and make them know; this storm is not forever. In Jesus Name, I pray. Amen!

The Fine Art of Gifting

I can see it now as though it were happening today in my own house. Charlie and Hudie would be surreptitiously kneeling in front of the meager little pile of gifts, carefully (so as not to be seen by Mother) lifting each one, giving it a little shake and a bit of a squeeze, then placing it back in its carefully thought-out position. And the conjecturing ("a conclusion deduced by surmise or guesswork"— *Webster's Dictionary*) would begin. The volume of which would increase to the point that the one they hoped would not know what was going on would be alerted.

"What are you boys doing?"

Then would come the age-old, tried-and-tested answer, "Nothing."

"I know what you're doing. Get away from those presents and leave them alone."

"Aw, Momma! We're just trying to guess what's in 'em."

The mystique—one knowing and the rest wondering—is largely what makes gift giving or gifting the pleasure that it is. Adults enjoy the charade too.

"France," my father said, "Get me two or three boxes, each one bigger than the other."

It seemed he had bought Mother a new wristwatch, so I helped him do the wrapping. First was the box with the beautiful new watch in it, then that wrapped box went into a larger box, which was also wrapped, sometimes pots and pans, a bottle of dish soap, or anything to add weight and disguise to the package. Then the grand finale was a box so large that it barely could clear the door. So the box in a box was placed in a box and wrapped. And of course, when Mother was opening all these boxes, Dad was sitting off to the side with a delightful gleam in his eye, urging Mother to "guess again." Oh, what fun it was to be in the Mason's house in those days.

But, God, however, was the very best of all at gifting. More than fun, more than the excitement and anticipation, indeed, much more than looking on with joy and happiness as the gift is opened, there is the obvious manifestation of love. Look at the process of discovery and the presentation of His best gift ever:

> And Joseph went into Judaea, unto the city of David, which is called Bethlehem; To be taxed with Mary his espoused wife, being great with child. And so it was, that, while they were there, the days were accomplished that she should be delivered. And she brought forth her firstborn son, and wrapped him in swaddling clothes, and laid him in a manger.
>
> And there were shepherds abiding in the field, And, lo, the angel of the Lord came, and the glory of the Lord shone round about them: And the angel said unto them, Fear not: for, behold, I bring you good tidings of great joy. For unto you is born this day in the city of David a Saviour, which is Christ the Lord. And this shall be a sign unto you; Ye shall find the babe wrapped in swaddling clothes, lying in a manger. (Luke 2:4–20)

"A baby! Swaddling clothes for wrapping paper! A stable? Are you kidding me! I was hoping to get a king, maybe kinda like Solomon used to be, remember? This is all I got? A baby in diapers! Cows and sheep?"

And someone said, "My child, don't judge the package by how it is wrapped! You might be surprised what you will find if you just open it!"

A Mother's Hiding Place

December 23 is my beloved Mother's birthday; and my thoughts are gentle. There should always be room in our hearts for expressions of tenderness and love for the one who carried us near her heart for many months and then beyond—way beyond.

It was she who spoke in Sunday Night testimony service when her youngest son was barely ten years old. Her words fell like sledge-hammer blows of conviction upon my heart as she told the audience of her thankfulness that two of her boys were serving the Lord: "But would you help me pray for my eldest and my youngest (*wham*!) sons that they would come to God before it's too late (*wham* again!)?"

I burst into tears, bending low in my seat as I wept. It was she who pressed her handkerchief into my hand, whispering, "Francis, why don't you go on up to the altar so we can pray with you."

It was her that I heard praying in her bedroom one afternoon when I was about fifteen or sixteen. She called my name out to God, asking the Lord to not let me grow cold and rebellious (*wham*!). She did not know that I left the house and went out to my "hiding place" behind the garage and wept and cried and prayed.

The mother of Jesus was exalted by the messenger of God. The angel said Mary was highly favored, blessed among women. She was just a young woman, a girl really. Mary didn't quite know how to respond and, understandably, was a bit fearful. We all might be a bit fearful, too, were we to find an angel speaking to us. The angel was quick to say, "Fear not, Mary: for thou hast found favor with God."

God's favor does not guarantee painless days, no sorrow. Waiting for the consolation (the comfort) of Israel was a man whose name *was* Simeon; and the Holy Ghost was upon him. And he came by the Spirit into the temple. And when the parents brought in the child Jesus to do for him after the custom of the law, then he took him up in his arms and blessed God. And Simeon blessed them and said unto Mary, his mother, "Behold, this child is set for the fall and rising again of many in Israel; Yea, a sword shall pierce through thy own soul also." (Luke 2:22–35).

> When Jesus was twelve years old, his parents went up to Jerusalem for the feast of Passover. And when they had fulfilled the days, they returned, not knowing Jesus was still in Jerusalem. They assumed he was with kinfolks also returning on the journey. But they went the entire first day on their journey before they missed him. They began seeking him among their kinsfolk and acquaintance. And when they found him not, they turned back again to Jerusalem, seeking him. Finally, he was found in the temple. And when they saw him, they were amazed. And his mother said unto him, "Son, why hast thou thus dealt with us? Behold, thy father and I have sought thee sorrowing." And he said unto them, "How is it that ye sought me? wist ye not that I must be about my Father's business?" And they understood not the saying which he spake unto them. And he went home with them, and came to Nazareth, and was subject unto them: but his mother kept all these sayings in her heart. (Luke 2:42–51)

I suppose, every mother has a place in her heart where she hides the secret communications with God about her children. This is as it should be. Don't banish it from your heart. After all, Mom, you carried him/her in your heart before they were born. Keep praying for your children. One might be standing, listening outside your door!

Shepherds and Angels

So, there they were. It was obvious something very unusual was happening among the clusters of houses and dwellings of the little village of Bethlehem. It was not even a stand-alone village, for it was but 5.5 miles from Jerusalem. There were often various temple events that drew out-of-town travelers to Jerusalem, hence some of the overflow crowd seeking lodging invariably made their way to the dusty little streets of Bethlehem. For sure, the prophet Micah did not exaggerate when he said the village was small.

An overflow crowd seeking lodging in this little village was in for some difficulties. Hostels were not plenteous; and householders willing to put up travelers for the night were few also. Rumor had it that the inn was running almost at capacity, and it wasn't dusk yet.

Adding to the chaos of a mobile society, even though it was temporary, was the required additional burden of animals and the necessary provender and water needed to care for them. One could only hope that the shepherds watching over their flocks in the growing darkness had been able to find water and a meadow of grass for them to graze at sunrise.

It was told that there was a band of shepherds holding their flock in a tight little group. (You just never knew when an evening wolf or even a lion or bear would come in close enough to frighten the flock.) When those large predators became hungry, their level of boldness increased exponentially. But as I started to say, it was told that there was a band of shepherds holding their flock close when (now you may not believe this, but just hear me out. I'm telling it just like it was told to me) the angel of the Lord came upon them, and the glory of the Lord shone round about them. And the shepherds were really frightened.

And the angel said unto the shepherds, "Don't be afraid, man, I've got some really awesome news for you. You are gonna really be glad to hear this because it is good news for everybody. Listen. Get a load of this: Unto you is born this day in the city of David a Savior, which is Christ the Lord. And this is the proof you need to look for. You will find the baby wrapped in swaddling clothes, lying in a manger. No, wait! What I'm telling you is true. The baby is lying in a manger. Okay. Okay. She was preg—uh, great—with child, and there was no room at the inn. The stable was the best the guy could do. Honest!"

And suddenly, there was with this angel, a whole bunch of these heavenly creatures, praising God and saying, "Glory to God in the highest, and on earth peace and good will toward men."

And then they were gone. Just like that. And that was all it took. Those shepherds said, "Let us now go into Bethlehem and see if this really did happen. Let's see if it really was the Lord speaking to us about something, which has come to pass, which He has made known unto us."

And they came with haste and found Mary and Joseph and the babe lying in a manger.

And the Shepherds Let Loose

And suddenly there was with the angel a multitude of the heavenly host praising God, and saying, Glory to God in the highest, and on earth peace, good will toward men. And it came to pass, as the angels were gone away from them into heaven, the shepherds said one to another, Let us now go even unto Bethlehem, and see this thing which is come to pass, which the Lord hath made known unto us. And the shepherds returned, glorifying and praising God for all the things that they had heard and seen, as it was told unto them.

—Luke 2:13–15, 20 (KJV)

At once the angel was joined by a huge angelic choir singing God's praises: Glory to God in the heavenly heights, Peace to all men and women on earth who please him. As the angel choir withdrew into heaven, the sheepherders talked it over. "Let's get over to Bethlehem as fast as we can and see for ourselves what God has revealed to us." The sheepherders returned and let loose, glorifying and praising God for everything they had heard and seen. It turned out exactly the way they'd been told!

—Luke 2:13–20 (MSG)

What man of you, having an hundred sheep, if he lose one of them, doth not leave the ninety and nine in the wilderness, and go after that which is lost, until he find it? And when he hath found *it,* he layeth *it* on his shoulders, rejoicing. And when he cometh home, he calleth together *his* friends and neighbours, saying unto them, Rejoice with me; for I have found my sheep which was lost. I say unto you, that likewise joy shall be in heaven over one sinner that repenteth, more than over ninety and nine just persons, which need no repentance.

—Luke 15:4–7 (KJV)

Either what woman having ten pieces of silver, if she lose one piece, doth not light a candle, and sweep the house, and seek diligently till she find *it?* And when she hath found *it,* she calleth *her* friends and *her* neighbours together, saying, Rejoice with me; for I have found the piece which I had lost. Likewise, I say unto you, there is joy in the presence of the angels of God over one sinner that repenteth.

—Luke 15:8–10 (KJV)

But the father said to his servants, Bring forth the best robe, and put *it* on him; and put a ring on his hand, and shoes on *his* feet: And bring hither the fatted calf, and kill *it;* and let us eat, and be merry: And they began to be merry. Now his elder son came and drew nigh to the house, he heard musick and dancing.

—Luke 15:22–25 (KJV)

When the lost is found, rejoice! When the prodigal comes home, throw a party! Kill the fatted calf! When the long-anticipated Savior of the world is born, cut loose! Join the choir; sing with the angels. The words of the song are easy to learn" "Glory to God in the highest, and on earth peace, good will toward men." Those words are deeply moving, truly expressive of God's remedy for needy man. Sing and rejoice!

"Glory to God in the highest, and on earth peace, good will toward men. Amen. Amen. Amen."

God Works

And we know that all things work together for
good to them that love God, to them who are the
called according to *his* purpose.

—Romans 8:28

Perhaps you have heard me speak of the sign art on the wall
of my office that says in stylized print, *God works.* If you look very
closely, you can see hidden amongst its own smallness these words:
"In all things, God works for good through those who love Him."
The artistic quotation is a bit skewed from the KJV, but for the most
part, the meaning comes through.

Coming through in a stronger sense, as I sit here writing and
looking at the artwork, is the part of the message that says, "Through
those who love Him." Considering my insignificance and His great-
ness, His work is extremely difficult. Yet He does it. I have the problem of many men (i.e., I'm all thumbs.) Manual dexterity is not one
of my high-efficiency achievements. However, I must admit that
Gloria does require me to always thread her sewing needles, which I
am able to accomplish with the aid of a large magnifying glass.

Through the miracle of minimal-invasive surgeries, such as lap-
aroscopic surgery, man can now operate within the abdomen of a
patient without the extreme incision wounds, scars, severe bleeding,
etc. With advancement of technology, he can enter the brain cavity
and surgically attempt to repair damage to the brain. And most people, believers, or nonbelievers, will readily acknowledge the sover-
eignty of God in all of this. I thank God for surgeons and physicians
who have God-given skills to perform these awesome, wonderful,

and frightening tasks. But there is yet a more advanced work that is available for the wholeness of humanity.

> And ye are complete in him, which is the head of all principality and power: In whom also ye are circumcised with the circumcision made without hands. Buried with him in baptism, wherein also ye are risen with *him* through the faith of the operation of God, who hath raised him from the dead.

Let's look at an expanded statement of this from the translation called The Message:

> Everything of God gets expressed in him, so you can see and hear him clearly. You don't need a telescope, a microscope, or a horoscope to realize the fullness of Christ, and the emptiness of the universe without him. When you come to him, that fullness comes together for you, too. His power extends over everything. If it's an initiation ritual you're after, you've already been through it by submitting to baptism. Going under the water was a burial of your old life; coming up out of it was a resurrection, God raising you from the dead as he did Christ. Think of it! All sins forgiven, the slate wiped clean, that old arrest warrant canceled and nailed to Christ's cross. (Colossians 2:9–15)

I tell you, in every situation of your life, *God works* if you let Him.

"Knock! Knock!"

"Who's there?"

"It's me, *Jesus*! I'm here to work for you today! May I come in?"

Open your heart and let Him in. He will remove your sorrow and sin. Jesus will be your dearest friend. So open your heart, and let

Him come in. Take His hand; take His nail-scarred hand. He will show you the way. He may not pass this way again. So open your heart, and let Him come in!

About the Author

Francis Mason was born in Visalia, located in the vast San Joaquin Valley of central California. The author does not hesitate to embellish his writings with events taken from the many experiences associated with living in a huge rural setting where the opportunities for a young lad to explore and go on an adventure were in abundance.

After graduating from Mt. Whitney High School, he married his high school sweetheart in 1962. Their two daughters have given them seven grandchildren and eight greats (with two more on the way). Shortly after their wedding, they began a lifetime of ministry, which has spanned over fifty-eight years and counting. This ministry has included traveling as an evangelist, pastoring in four churches, including the past thirty-five years in Surrey, British Columbia,

Canada. He has served in executive leadership positions in the United Pentecostal Church International and as a member of three Districts. He is retiring from the International Global Mission Board after twenty-five years of service. His role in Global Missions included travel in Europe, Africa, Asia, South America, Central America, and the Caribbean.

While serving as the Executive Presbyter for the UPC of Canada, he was given the challenge of editing and publishing a magazine, which was to feature Canadian content only. Over the next twelve years, with the help of God and his good wife Gloria, this "short-term" project became a twenty-four-page full-color magazine with a circulation reaching into every province and/or territory of Canada as well as several outlets in the United States. And thanks to Global Missions, all of the more than 175 missionary units around the world received one of the Canadian *Focus* magazines in their mailbox every month.

When asked what happens after his retirement, Mason says, "I plan to rest, write, read, flirt with my sweetheart, play with my greats, and keep on enjoying the blessings of God—not necessarily in that order."

CPSIA information can be obtained
at www.ICGtesting.com
Printed in the USA
BVHW050610200622
640037BV00001B/4

9 781685 175993